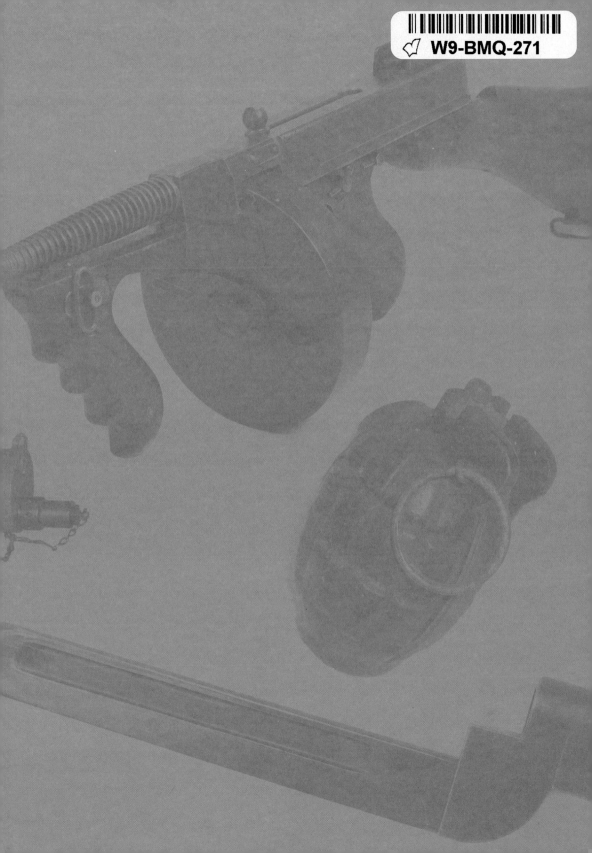

Fifty Weapons
That Changed the Course of

History

written by Joel Levy

A FIREFLY BOOK

Published by Firefly Books Ltd. 2014

Copyright © 2014 Quid Publishing

First printing

Publisher Cataloging-in-Publication Data (U.S.)

A CIP record for this title is available from the
Library of Congress

**Library and Archives Canada Cataloguing
in Publication**

A CIP record for this title is available from
Library and Archives Canada

Published in the United States by
Firefly Books (U.S.) Inc.
P.O. Box 1338, Ellicott Station
Buffalo, New York 14205

Published in Canada by
Firefly Books Ltd.
50 Staples Avenue, Unit 1
Richmond Hill, Ontario L4B 0A7

Printed in China

Conceived, designed, and produced by
Quid Publishing
Level 4, Sheridan House
114 Western Road
Hove BN3 1DD
England

Interior design: Tony Seddon

Fifty Weapons

That Changed the Course of

History

written by Joel Levy

FIREFLY BOOKS

To DON IN APPRECIATION. R.TEMPLEFOX

CONTENTS

50

The supposed deathbed lament of John Napier, who protested that "for the ruin and overthrow of man, there were too many devices already framed," articulates a common distaste for the application of technological and scientific genius to the business of killing. (Napier's protestations ring hollow for the man himself, who was driven by sectarian antipathy to contrive a host of strange and terrible "devices for the ruin and overthrow of man," including "devices of sailing under the water ... a closed and fortified carriage to bring arquebusiers into the midst of an enemy ... [and] a kind of shot for artillery ... calculated to clear a field of four miles' circumference of all living things above a foot in height: by it, he said, the inventor could destroy 30,000 Turks, without the hazard of a single Christian." From *Domestic Annals of Scotland*, Robert Chambers.)

Although this book is not intended as a glorification of warfare and killing, it celebrates the art and technology of weapons, and admires the creativity and ingenuity of weapon makers, ancient and modern, renowned and anonymous. Through an examination of 50 of the most significant weapons in history, it explores how technology has changed warfare, and by extension the rest of human history.

War may not be the most important determinant of the course of history — its degree of influence compared to, say, economy, geography, or individual actors, is subject to debate — but clearly it is one of the primary factors, and perhaps the one with the most apparent and easily traceable impact. It thus follows that the tools of warfare are important factors in history, especially when developments in these tools, whether incremental or revolutionary, have a material impact on the outcome of battle. So although this book looks at specific weapons in detail, exploring technical aspects of their development, mechanisms, and effects, its purview extends much farther, to encompass grand themes of history, epochal changes, and underlying currents. Through the history of the spear, for instance, we can glimpse the story of human colonization of the planet (see page 12),

"When he was desired by a friend in his last illness to reveal the contrivance [of a secret weapon], his answer was that, for the ruin and overthrow of man, there were too many devices already framed, which if he could make to be fewer, he would with all his might endeavour to do so; and that therefore seeing the malice and rancour rooted in the heart of mankind will not suffer them to diminish, by any new conceit of his the number of them should never be increased."

SIR THOMAS URQUHART'S REPORT OF THE LAST WORDS OF JOHN NAPIER, SCOTTISH MATHEMATICIAN AND WEAPONS INVENTOR

whereas the technical details of the stirrup may have had profound consequences for the course of Western civilization (see page 44).

The choice of topics covered must, inevitably, be contentious and, to a degree, arbitrary: history has not been altered by exactly 50 weapons, no more or fewer. In particular the list has been composed within some fuzzy constraints, based on my personal and not always consistent interpretation of the term "weapon." I have excluded most vehicles, especially ships and planes, on the basis that these are less weapons and more platforms for weapons; but on the other hand I have included tanks and the horse. I have tried to include only specific devices or implements, excluding more general concepts such as iron, money, or railroads, all of which can claim to have been the primary determinants of military success at one time or another; on the other hand, I have included smallpox and stirrups.

Each entry is dated and categorized. The dates given do not necessarily reflect the invention/origins of the weapon, but refer to its heyday — the start of the time or period when it had its greatest impact. Sometimes this comes long after the weapon first came into being: hand grenades, for instance, date back to the earliest beginnings of gunpowder technology, but arguably became most influential as a military technology from the First World War onward. The pike — a long-hafted blade weapon — is essentially a spear, and hence its origins date back to earliest prehistory, but its glory days as a weapon did not come until the Renaissance "pike and shot" era of the 16th through 17th centuries. The categories used to describe each weapon — social, technical, political, and tactical — are likely to be as contentious as the contents list itself. Broadly speaking they describe the main ways in which the weapon impacted on history. Any battlefield weapon can be argued to have tactical significance, but some weapons have impacts beyond the battlefield; the horse and stirrup, for instance, had transformative effects on society and the economy, whereas the importance of ballistic missiles is probably more political than military.

50

01

Inventor(s):

Homo habilis

STONE AX

Type:

Hand weapon

Social ■

Political

Tactical

Technical ■

" … for over a million years, [the hand ax] was literally the cutting edge of technology. It accompanied our ancestors through half of their history, and was the main reason they spread first across Africa and then across the world."

NEIL MACGREGOR, *A HISTORY OF THE WORLD IN 100 OBJECTS*

c. 2–3 million years ago

The stone ax was probably the first weapon devised by members of the genus *Homo*. Its appearance and development have been closely tied in with the evolution of mankind, and it has perhaps had a greater effect on human history than any other weapon in these pages. Yet the object typically encountered in a museum labeled as a "stone ax" may well be nothing of the kind, and uncertainty surrounds the nature and purpose of many examples of this class of object.

Here comes a chopper

As befits perhaps the oldest technology on Earth, the stone ax is not a single, unchanging tool; it evolved and diversified through many different forms and functions. The earliest examples are scarcely recognizable to the untrained eye, as they appear to be simply broken rocks. In fact, these are the first stone tools created by our earliest human ancestors, *Homo habilis*, and also used by their successors, such as *Homo erectus*. Called Oldowan tools, after the Olduvai Gorge site in northern Tanzania where they were first discovered, these early axes are also known as "choppers" and are the simplest to construct. Any fresh break of a

rock of flint or similar stone will tend to leave a sharp edge along the fracture line, and *Homo habilis* may have deliberately created choppers by striking rocks together, or simply used naturally broken rocks. The resulting choppers can be used to cut, to scrape, or, presumably, to bash other hominins, making them the first stone weapons as well as tools.

Oldowan tools were succeeded by what are known as Acheulian (or Acheulean) tools, after the Saint-Acheul site in northern France. Associated with later hominins such as *Homo erectus*, *Homo neanderthalis*, and early *Homo sapiens*, Acheulian tools show evidence of highly developed stonecraft. Expert flint knappers crafted pear-shaped hand axes by striking flakes from either side of a core. This created useful smaller blades (with the flakes) and a more substantial tool with the core as a hand ax. These are so named because they were the wrong shape for hafting (being fixed to a haft or handle), and would have been held

Oldowan choppers from the archaeological site of Melka Kunture, in Ethiopia.

directly in the hand. The hands of prehistoric people may have been sturdier and hardened by calluses, or perhaps they used a piece of leather as a hand shield like modern hand ax wielders. In fact, there is some question over the extent to which the true purposes of "hand axes" can ever be known. Perhaps they were not used as axes or tools at all, but had ceremonial or economic value? Accordingly, they are now often called "bifaces," a purely descriptive term.

The Acheulian tool "industry" reached great heights of sophistication and skill. One remarkable feature of some periods and areas of biface production is that all the examples adhere to the same proportions between length and width, and that this ratio is what the ancient Greeks came to call the Golden Ratio or Golden Section. This is the ratio produced by cutting a line such that the shorter section is in the same proportion to the longer section as the longer section is to the whole. It works out — for width/height — as roughly 0.61. Given that prehistoric flint knappers had no written instructions to follow, the finding suggests that they must have been capable of conceptualizing proportionality to some degree.

Celts and true axes

Acheulian bifaces persisted for a remarkably long time, still being made and used by anatomically modern humans around 50,000 years ago, but in the period known as the Upper Paleolithic Transition, c. 40,000 years ago, human cultural evolution appears to have accelerated and stone tools changed too. Bifaces evolved into more, increasingly specialized forms, such as long blades for spears or barbs for harpoons. Hafting of stone tools probably became more common and widespread, but it seems that hafted axes only arrived relatively late, around 30,000 years ago, with hafted "true" axes not common in northern Europe, for instance, until around 10,000 years ago.

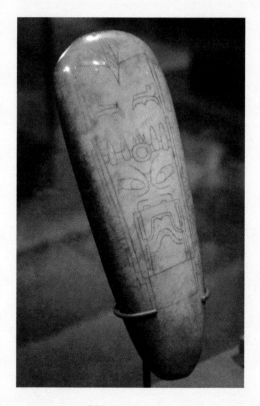

This inscribed celt comes from the Olmec culture of Central America, showing the wide temporal and geographical range of celt manufacture.

During the Upper Paleolithic, anatomically modern humans began to place greater value on their axes/bifaces. Whereas most Neanderthal tools are made from local flint, Upper Paleolithic *H. sapiens* would travel 100 miles (161 km) or more to find decent sources of flint for their tools. By Neolithic times ax heads evolved into objects of great beauty, known as celts, some examples of which are crafted from semiprecious stones and have been polished with sand. These were probably not intended for use, instead possessing ritual, economic, or perhaps purely aesthetic significance.

Haft time

Hafting makes use of the force-multiplying mechanical principle of leverage. An ax head swung on the end of a haft moves faster and delivers more force on impact, as well as increasing the distance between ax wielder and target. This made the ax more potent for hunting and combat, and more effective for chopping. In fact, it may have been the need to chop wood to clear areas of forest in the Mesolithic era and early Neolithic that led to wider adoption of hafted axes.

Ax hafts would probably have been made of wood, bone, or antler, with the heads fixed on with plant or animal fibers and early glues such as birch tar. Stone ax heads with bored holes for hafts appeared relatively late; in northern Europe, for instance, they came around the same time as the first metal ax blades. These bored stone axes have been called "battle axes," but the distinction between battle and tool ax depends on the length of the haft, and these have not survived from prehistoric times. A battle ax generally has a haft around half the length of an adult arm, with tool ax hafts being shorter (or longer for specialized tasks). Battle ax haft length maximizes leverage and fighting distance without sacrificing handling.

Ax factor

Arguably the simplest weapon in human history, the stone ax can also claim to have been the most important, with transformative consequences for human evolution. The adoption of stone tools radically increased early man's ability to hunt and process bigger animal carcasses, providing skins, sinews, and bone parts for use and boosting the meat content of his diet. With more protein and calories available for less effort, this dietary change led to anatomical and physiological changes, such as smaller jawbones and smaller intestines, which in turn made possible the evolution of bigger brains and social intelligence.

Stone axes also increased human control over the environment, whether through clearing forest or shaping wood. For instance, the stone adze (a relative of the ax) could be used to shape a tree trunk into a log canoe, making marine travel possible.

The impact of the ax as a weapon of war is less clear. Estimates by archaeologists vary greatly but it is now generally accepted that the Neolithic and Bronze Ages were fairly violent, with widespread warfare; axes would have played their part as weapons and spoils of war.

02

Inventor(s):

Homo erectus* or *Homo heidelbergensis

SPEAR

Type:
Pole weapon

Social
Political
Tactical
Technical

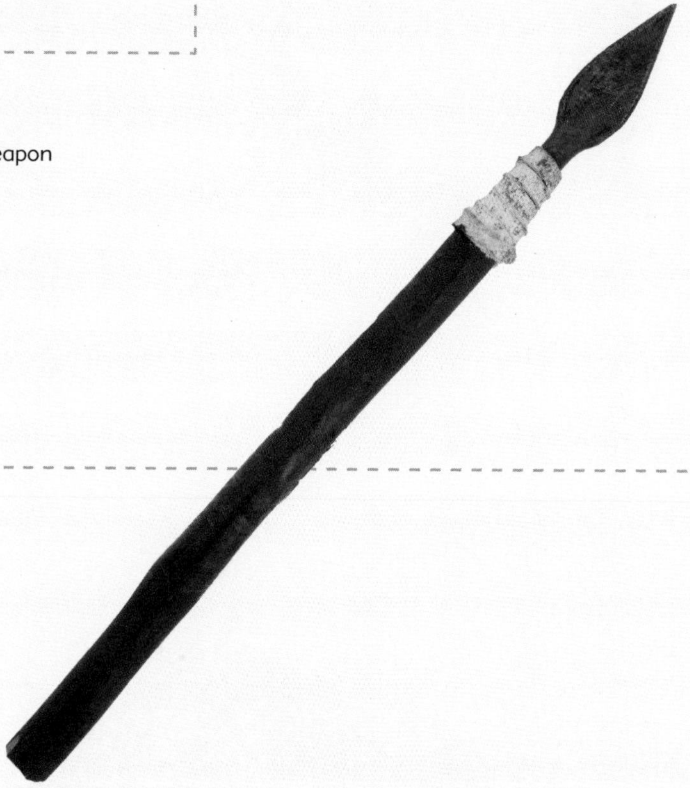

At least 400,000 years ago

The spear is the only universal weapon; every culture/civilization has used it. This was probably inevitable given the simplicity of its most essential form: a pointy stick. Dating the origins of such a simple technology is impossible, but c. 400,000 years ago is a reasonable guess, if its emergence as an engineered weapon is set at the point when fire was first used to harden the sharpened end of a stick. Although the first evidence of hominin-made fire dates to 790,000 years ago, the mainstream consensus is that the widespread controlled use of fire dates to not much earlier than 400,000 years ago.

It may have been *Homo erectus* or *Homo heidelbergensis* who first adapted sticks into weapons of war, although it is probable that cruder spears (i.e., broken branches) were used millions of years ago; chimpanzees have been observed using sticks as tools and even weapons. In fact, the oldest surviving spears date to precisely around the time of the first controlled use of fire, coming from a 380,000 to 400,000-year-old site in a cave near Schöningen in Germany, and believed to have been left by a group of late *Homo heidelbergensis*. The spears were 6 to 8 feet (1.8–2.4 m) long and sharpened at both ends, although without stone tips. They were found alongside the butchered remains of 10 horses, and so were presumably hunting weapons.

Flint spearheads

The next leap in spear evolution was the manufacture of flint spear points to be fixed to shafts of wood or bone, and these appear as part of the Mousterian flint industry (from c. 300 to 30,000 years ago) traditionally associated with Neanderthal man. It is only during the cultural and technical "great leap" of the Upper Paleolithic transition (c. 40,000 years ago) that anatomically modern *Homo sapiens* began to make high-quality flint spearheads. These are delicate and often very beautiful artifacts, leaf-shaped, fluted, sometimes shouldered. They are precision-knapped to make them easier to haft, and to encourage the flow of blood from wounds.

Flint-tipped spears traveled the world with the expanding and exploring *Homo sapiens* population of the Upper Paleolithic. One of their most notable and distinctive expressions came in the shape of the Clovis tool industry. "Clovis peoples" is the name given to the first humans to settle the Americas widely. Originating in northeast Asia, they probably crossed a land bridge over the Bering Strait and migrated down through Canada into North America around 15,000 years ago (reaching the bottom of South America only around 3,000 years later). Their name derives from the New Mexico town where their distinctive spear tips — known as Clovis points — were first dug up in 1936. These beautifully engineered spear

points are found in the bottom layer of sites across North America, often in association with the animals they were used to kill. Clovis spears probably accounted for — or at least contributed significantly to — the demise of much of the American megafauna, such as mammoths, giant sloths, and so on.

Metal spears

Stone spear tips continued to be used in pre-industrial cultures around the world until modern times; the Normans in France still used them as late as the eighth century CE. But the Bronze Age saw the development of the spear as the primary weapon of war and the evolution of the spear to its classical form. Wood such as ash, which is strong with a longitudinal grain, was used for a long shaft without grips, handles, or other interruptions. The tip could be narrow or broad and leaf-shaped, depending on culture, fashion, and intended use. The butt of the spear might be fitted with a butt-spike or ferrule, to enable it to be planted and so that both ends could be useful.

Metal spears and the way in which they were used changed little from the Bronze Age to the classical era. The oldest known historical document, the Stele of Vultures, is a Sumerian artifact commemorating the victory of Eannatum, King of Lagash, over a neighboring city c. 2450 BCE. It shows a regiment of helmeted Sumerian soldiers marching in serried ranks, brandishing tall spears and clutching rectangular shields. There is not much difference in appearance between them and a phalanx of Greek hoplites or a legion of Romans, up to 3,000 years later.

The hoplite dory

It was in the hands of these hoplites that the spear enjoyed its finest hour in history. Hoplites were armored citizen infantry from the Greek city-states. As they had to provide their own expensive arms and armor, they tended to be the elite of Greek society. Although named for

" ... few [of the Germans] use swords or long lances. They carry a spear (*framea* is their name for it), with a narrow and short head, but so sharp and easy to wield that the same weapon serves, according to circumstances, for close or distant conflict."

TACITUS, *GERMANIA*, C. 100 CE

Spear- and shield-bearing troops shown marching in close formation on the Stele of Vultures.

base, maximizing the deployed length of the shaft. The *sarouter* was also a vital secondary weapon, enabling both ends of the dory to be lethal and supplying a backup if the spear broke or when close-quarters combat made it hard to wield the spear tip.

Similar debates rage over the grip that the hoplites would have used. Most ancient depictions show them wielded with an overarm grip (i.e., held above the shoulder), which may have been necessary if the phalanx was to present an unbroken shield wall frontage. On the other hand, such a grip is extremely tiring and unwieldy, whereas an underarm grip allows more control and makes it easier to hold the dory near its base. Again, reenactors offer opposing conclusions from their firsthand experience.

Wielding their dorys, the hoplites of ancient Greece forged powerful city-states and defeated waves of Persian invaders in the fifth century BCE. In the fourth century BCE, Alexander the Great used the phalanx to spearhead his conquest of the known world, equipping his Macedonians with the *sarissa*, a spear that was up to 23 feet (7 m) long and had to be wielded with two hands, with a small shield buckled onto the person of the spearman.

Eventually, the Roman legions overcame the might of the phalanx, skillfully using tactics that helped the *pilum* (javelin) and *gladius* (short-bladed sword, see page 40) outmatch the dory. But spears continued to be a vital element of the arsenal of many cultures.

his *hoplon*, or large shield of wood faced with a bronze sheet, the hoplite's main weapon was his dory, a long spear. Exactly how long is the topic of much debate. Herodotus emphasizes that the hoplite dory outranged the Persians' shorter spears, and many authorities put the length at 10 feet (3 m) or more. Modern-day reenactors bring personal experience to bear on the debate, but even they cannot agree. Reenactor Nikolas Lloyd, for instance, claims that anything over 8 feet (2.4 m) is unmanageably heavy, whereas the hoplite reenactors of the website 4hoplites. com claim that 9 feet (2.7 m) is practical.

Factors that affected the balance of the dory, and thus its potential length, included the size of the leaf-shaped *aichme* (blade), which may have been relatively small and affixed to the thin end of a tapered shaft, minimizing the weight at the tip. Meanwhile, a heavy butt-spike, known as a *sarouter*, would have counterbalanced the blade so that the spear could be held nearer the

SPEAR

03

Inventor(s):

Paleolithic Africans

BOW AND ARROW

Type:
Projectile weapon system

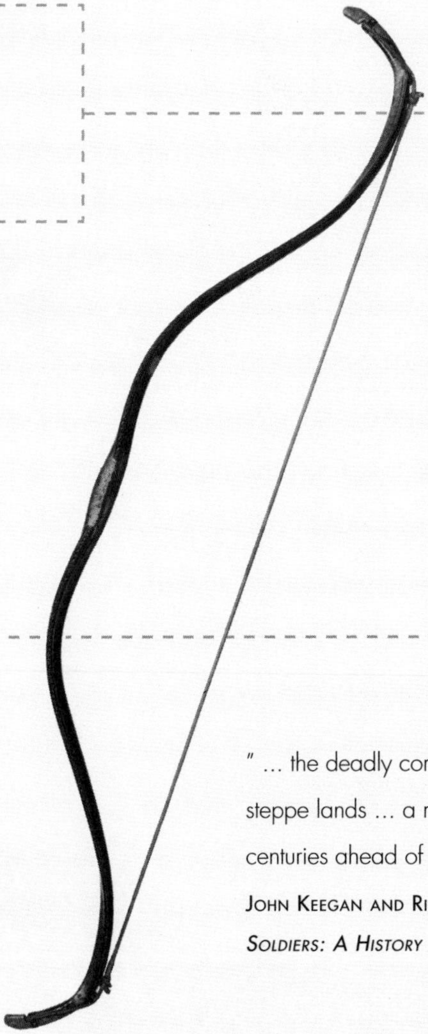

Social
Political
Tactical
Technical

" ... the deadly composite bow of the steppe lands ... a miracle of technology centuries ahead of its time ..."

JOHN KEEGAN AND RICHARD HOLMES,
SOLDIERS: A HISTORY OF MEN IN BATTLE

c. 60,000 BCE

Like the atlatl (see page 20), the bow and arrow constitute more than just a new weapon or even a technological advance. Their creation marked the development of cognitive and social capabilities qualitatively different from what had gone before, and their impact profoundly altered human evolution at every level. With the bow, humans had the ability to apply deadly force from a distance, making relatively small, weak humans more powerful and more dangerous than any other animal. The bow would also transform intraspecies conflict, becoming a game-changing weapon of war, with developments in bow technology altering the course of history.

Arrowheads and bog bows

Bows were made from organic, biodegradable materials and hence there is a limit to how far back in the archaeological record they can be found: the oldest surviving bows are less than 10,000 years old (see below). Arrowheads, on the other hand, were sometimes made from stone, and evidence collected from Sibudu Cave, a cliff cave in northern KwaZulu-Natal, South Africa, suggests that humans living there were making arrows around 60,000 years ago. Researchers found stone points with impact and hafting marks that suggest that they were used in projectiles rather than spears. They even found traces of plant-resin glues used to help fix the points to their shafts, evidence of composite tool production indicating a high level of cognitive ability. It is impossible to say for sure whether these projectile points belonged to arrows or atlatl darts, but mainstream opinion is the former.

The earliest unequivocal evidence comes from preserved bows, and due to the prevalence of conditions that favor preservation and the relative intensity of archaeology, the majority of these have been found in Europe. The oldest undisputed bows in the world are the Mesolithic Holmegaard bows from a peat bog in Denmark, dated to about 9,200 years ago; they are made from elm. In the Neolithic era, there is evidence of the use of bows in warfare. At the Crickley hill fort in England, the distribution of flint arrowheads vividly recreates the course of battle in around 3000 BCE, with concentrations of hundreds of heads around the entrance gates.

Self bows to composites

These early bows, known as self bows, were of the simplest design, made from a single piece of wood. The very first were probably of springy green wood, but as bow technology advanced bow makers learned to season their woods, using strong, elastic woods such as ash, oak, elm, and yew. They learned to cut the wood so that the more flexible sapwood lay on the face of the bow (confusingly known as the back, see box on page 19) whereas the tougher, more compressible heartwood lay on the belly or inside of the bow. As early as 3600 BCE (the early Bronze Age in Europe), a bow from Lake

Mongol warriors shooting their bows from the saddle in a 14th-century Persian miniature.

Ledro in northern Italy demonstrates a recursive design where the tips of the limbs curve back toward the front.

Bows seem to have gone out of fashion in Bronze Age Europe but bow design advanced in the Middle East and Asia, with metal tools making it easier to work wood and providing better arrowheads. The greatest advance, however, came with the development of composite materials for the bows. First came the "backed" bow, where strips of elastic bone or animal sinew were glued to the back of the wooden stave. Then came three-layered composite bows made from wood sandwiched between highly elastic sinew on the back of the bow and strongly compressible horn on the belly. Constructed with sophisticated techniques involving different glues, these composite bows packed greater strength and elasticity into a much smaller bow, allowing them to be wielded by men on horseback, transforming the horse warrior into a highly mobile missile launcher. The horse peoples of the steppe lands of Asia and eastern Europe mastered the art of archery from horseback, such as the Parthians with their famous Parthian shot, where the rider was able to turn all the way around in his saddle and release a shot in one direction as he rode off — out of harm's way — in the other.

The power of composite bows affected military history repeatedly. When ancient Egypt was invaded by the Hyksos peoples around 1720 BCE, their superior composite bow technology meant they outranged the self bows of the Egyptians by up to 200 yards (183 m). The Hyksos soon conquered Egypt. Later, composite bows helped the Parthians to fend off the encroaching Roman Empire for centuries, but the culmination of the synergy between composite bows and cavalry came with the Mongols.

These steppe warriors combined great skill in horsemanship and archery with sophisticated bow technology. Each rider was equipped with at least one short, composite, recurved bow of great power, giving a range of over 1,000 feet (305 m), complemented with a range of specialized arrows, each adapted for different tactical effects (e.g. armor-piercing, anti-horse, flaming, and so on). The Mongols developed battlefield tactics to suit these weapons, staying mobile, coordinating their maneuvers, keeping out of range of enemy weapons, feigning retreat, and so on. With their composite bows the Mongols humbled the armies of medieval Europe and their heavily armored knights.

THE BOW

[A] Upper limb
[B] Grip
[C] Lower limb
[D] Nock
[E] Bracing height

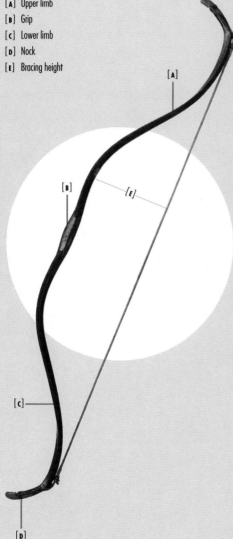

A bow has two limbs (upper and lower), either side of a central grip. The side facing away from the archer is called the back, the side facing the archer is the belly. Notches at the tips for fixing the bowstring are called nocks. The gap between the bow and the string when the bow is strung is called the *fistmele*, or bracing height.

A bow is a device for converting human work (in the sense of force applied over distance) into kinetic energy (to propel an arrow). You could simply throw an arrow, but then you would be wasting much of your energy in moving your arm, and more importantly you would be limited by the relatively small amount of force you can produce at any given moment. With a bow, you can exert this force over a longer period of time as you draw back the string — the bow is essentially a spring. The work you do is converted into mechanical or elastic potential energy in the bent bow, and when the string is released this potential energy is very rapidly converted into kinetic energy. Energy is put into the bow slowly, then transferred very fast into the arrow. In physics, such a device is known as a power amplifier.

KEY FEATURE:
THE COMPOSITE

The startling power to weight ratio of the composite bow derives from its sophisticated employment of materials science, although this concept was alien at the time of the bow's inception. Contemporary craftsmen blended experience and intuition in the combination of materials with complementing characteristics: horn for compressibility; sinew for elasticity.

04

Inventor(s):

Upper Paleolithic Europeans

ATLATL/SPEAR-THROWER

Social

Political

Tactical

Technical

Type:

Projectile weapon

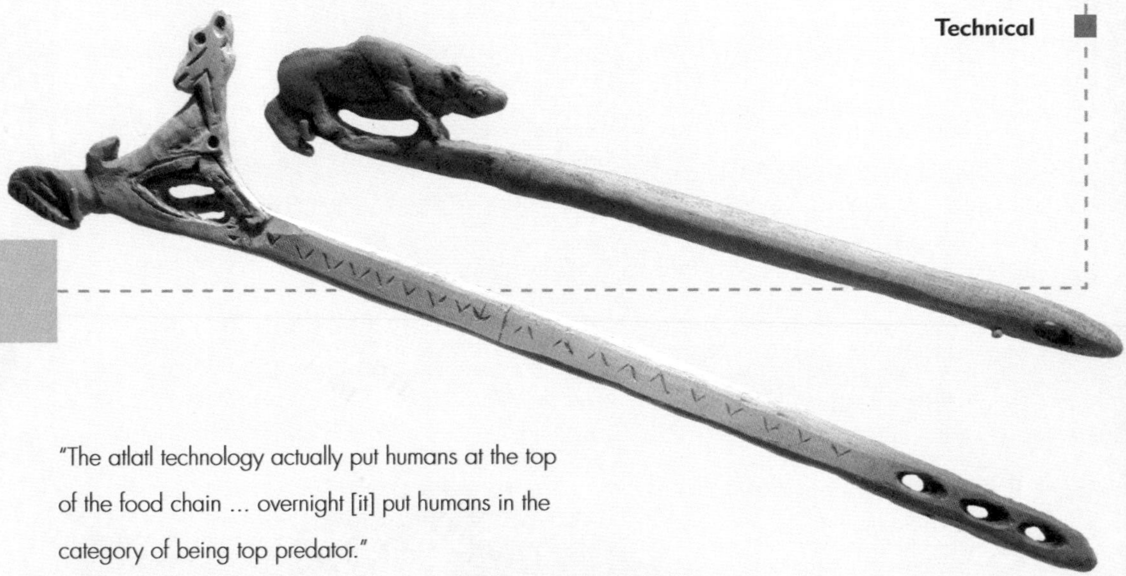

"The atlatl technology actually put humans at the top of the food chain ... overnight [it] put humans in the category of being top predator."

Bob Sizemore of SALT (Study of Ancient Lifeways and Technologies)

At least 17,500 years ago

The atlatl or spear-thrower is a missile-launching weapon that may be as old or older than the bow and arrow. Together with its associated projectile — usually known as a dart — it constituted the first weapons system. By applying the principle of mechanical advantage to a ranged weapon it transformed the ability and ambition of prehistoric hunters, and offered a tactical advantage to the user that practically leveled the playing field between Stone Age and early modern warriors as late as the 16th-century Spanish conquest of the Americas.

Many names, many places

The word *atlatl* comes from the Nahuatl language used by the Mexica, the American Indian inhabitants of the Valley of Mexico, generally known as the Aztecs. According to some sources it means "water-thrower"; apparently the Mexica used it to hunt wild fowl over lakes and marshes. The device itself has been found in prehistoric, historical, or present-day cultures on every continent except Antarctica and, intriguingly, Africa. Other names include spear- or dart-thrower, *woomera* or *miru* (transliterations of Australian Aboriginal terms), *propulseur* (French), *Speerschleuder* (German), and *estolica* (Spanish).

What is an atlatl?

An atlatl is simply a stick or board with a notch or projection at one end (typically known as a spur or hook). The user grasps the atlatl at the other end, and fits the butt of a dart, spear, or similar projectile to the spur or into the notch. The atlatl starts off lying flat along the forearm with the throwing arm bent at the elbow and brought up level with the ear. When the throwing arm is then brought forward and extended, the atlatl artificially extends the arm from the wrist. By giving a longer lever at the wrist, the atlatl thus multiplies the force produced by the flick or snap of the wrist that constitutes the final phase of the throwing movement. As the wrist comes forward at high speed, the spur of the atlatl is moving in an arc at a much higher speed, imparting great acceleration to the dart. According to John Whittaker of The World Atlatl Association:

> The throwing motion is the same as throwing a ball or a rock. The main difference is when you snap your wrist at the end of a pitch, your wrist provides a short lever arm while that same wrist snap with an atlatl provides a long lever, like adding another arm joint.

Making an atlatl is quite easy — any stick that forks near the base can be used. Simply cut one of the arms just above where the stick forks to create a "stubby arm," and bind string or tape around the end of the long arm that is farthest from where the stick forks; this will be the handle or grip, whereas the nub of the cut fork

will be the spur. According to the Prehistoric Archery and Atlatl Society, the ease of use of the device is inversely proportional to its simplicity: "the spear-thrower is the epitome of projectile simplicity but is rather tricky to use."

Once mastered, however, the atlatl can be devastating. According to Bob Sizemore of SALT (Study of Ancient Lifeways and Technologies), a dart launched from an atlatl has about 200% more energy than one thrown by hand alone. This can increase the achievable range — the world record distance for an atlatl throw is 848 feet (258 m). It also makes powerful throws far more accurate over shorter distances, which is seen by many as the key benefit of the atlatl as a weapon for both hunting and war. With an atlatl, quite heavy projectiles can be launched with great power and speed without sacrificing accuracy, so that, for instance, an atlatl of around 3 feet (1 m) can be used to launch a 5-foot (1.5 m) dart at 50 mph (80 kph). According to Sizemore, darts can even reach speeds of up to 170 mph (274 kph). The combination of weight and speed means that atlatl darts have great penetrating power, able to pierce the bodies of game animals or even puncture metal armor, as the conquistadors unhappily discovered during their wars with the Aztecs. Modern experimenters should take great care as even amateur attempts can penetrate through doors or cause lethal injury.

Dart invaders

Atlatls first appear in the archaeological record in Europe in the Upper (i.e., late) Paleolithic. The oldest surviving example belongs to the ancient culture known as the Solutrean, dating back to c. 21,000 to 15,000 years ago in what is now France and Spain, with multiple examples from the succeeding period, known as the Magdalenian, c. 15,000 years ago. These include some remarkably beautiful artifacts, such as the atlatl known as "*Le faon aux oiseaux*" from La Mas d'Azil archaeological site, which is made from reindeer bone and decorated with carved ibex and birds.

Atlatls appear in the archaeological record in the Americas c. 10,000 years ago, and the similarity in style between these Paleoamerican atlatls and the older European Solutrean ones has been used in support of the controversial "Solutrean hypothesis," which posits that the Americas were first peopled by prehistoric Europeans. The mainstream academic view is that the Americas were settled by Paleolithic Siberians, but there is no archaeological record of atlatls being used by them. It is also striking that there is no evidence of atlatl use in Africa. One important point to consider is that atlatls are made from perishable organic materials, primarily wood, bone, and antler, and it may be that they were in widespread use even before anatomically modern humans left Africa c. 90,000 years ago but that none have survived (it is possible, for instance, that large flint points usually described as "arrowheads," found in the Tunisian Sahara and dating to c. 50,000 years ago, may be from atlatl darts).

This might help account for their widespread distribution, from Australia to the Arctic, or it may simply be that such a relatively simple technology has been easy for different cultures to invent independently.

In North America the atlatl was largely superseded by the bow and arrow, although this process was slow, spanning the period 3000 BCE to 500 CE. In some places the two technologies coexisted, and the atlatl has some advantages over the bow — for instance, it can be used in wet weather when organic bowstrings can lose tension. In many parts of the world people practicing pre-industrial lifestyles still use them, or did up until the 20th century, such as Aboriginal Australians, Native American Aleuts, and Kuikuru Amazon Indians.

Depiction of a 19th-century Siberian Aleut using a spear-thrower to launch a harpoonlike dart.

Bannerstones

The field of atlatl studies is surprisingly controversial. There is some debate, for example, over whether the atlatl works by simple leverage, or acts like a bowstring, imparting elastic energy to the dart, which is stored by deformation (high-speed photographic studies suggest the former). There is related dispute over whether the velocity imparted to the dart is increased if the atlatl, dart, or both are designed to flex (again, studies suggest that flexibility may increase precision and/or compensate for flaws in technique, but does not affect velocity). But perhaps the greatest controversy is over the purpose of the stones often found alongside atlatls in North America, known as atlatl weights or bannerstones. These are not found associated with atlatls anywhere else in the world. It has been suggested they add momentum to the dart or help produce a smoother throw; it has also been suggested that they are used for the repair of darts or atlatls, and that they have purely ceremonial or social significance. Their sophisticated craftsmanship, high aesthetic value, and role as grave goods in some areas certainly suggests that they were not purely utilitarian.

05

Inventor(s):
West Asians

BRONZE AGE
SWORD

Type:

Bladed weapon

Social ■

Political

Tactical

Technical ■

c. 3000 BCE

The emblematic weapon of the pre-gunpowder age, the sword was a prestige weapon for most of its history, expensive to make and own, bestowing status and prestige on the bearer. Its existence depended on the discovery of metalworking. Stone blades had been honed and perfected to a fine degree, but the longest practical weapons that could be made from stone were short daggers and knives. Stone blades fractured too easily to maintain an edge, especially when sharpened, and anything longer than a dagger would be impractically heavy to wield.

Copper-cetic

Copper is a metal that occurs naturally in its pure form; it is also attractive, malleable, and corrosion-resistant. Humans learned to work with it as early as 9000 BCE, but the Chalcolithic or Copper Age did not begin in earnest until the organized production and use of copper began in Mesopotamia around 4500 BCE. Copper was made into weapons such as daggers and ax heads, although the softness of the metal means that historians question the effectiveness of such items; given the beauty and value of copper, it may be that these were often ceremonial items.

Copper was not well suited for slashing and cutting, but it was hard enough to give stabbing points, so copper blades were mainly daggers. The earliest swords on record are those found in 2003 at Arslantepe, in the Taurus mountains of Turkey. Archaeologists found nine blades dating back to about 3300 BCE (1,000 years older than the next oldest), which they describe as "swords." Ranging from 17.7 to 23.6 inches (45–60 cm) in length, they had blades and hilts cast as single pieces. Skeptics question whether these were swords as opposed to long daggers, but the Arslantepe blades were made from an alloy of arsenic and copper that, according to Marcella Frangipane, professor at the department of historical science, archaeology, and anthropology of antiquities of Rome University, "indicated great metallurgy skills. When forging the swords, arsenic was used as a deliberate alloying element in order to change the properties of copper and produce a stronger metal ... Their length ... leaves no doubt about their use."

A type of copper sword was common in ancient Egypt: the *khopesh*, or sickle-sword. The classic example of a design that appeared across the Middle East, the sickle-sword derived its form from the agricultural tool but was used in battle as a slashing weapon, and also as an executioner's blade. The Egyptian *khopesh* could be up to 23.6 inches (60 cm) long.

Khopesh, or sickle-sword, from the Levant, dating to the eighth century BCE, with a bronze blade decorated with electrum inlays.

"Achilles drew his keen blade, and struck [Lycaon] by the collarbone on his neck; he plunged his two-edged sword into him to the very hilt, whereon he lay at full length on the ground, with the dark blood welling from him till the earth was soaked."

HOMER, THE ILIAD, BOOK XXI

Men of bronze

The precise dividing line between dagger and sword depends on whether the blade is used for stabbing only or for slashing as well, but this is impossible to determine from archaeological finds. Length can also give clues — with the possible exception of the Egyptian *khopesh*, longer blades, 20 to 35 inches (51–89 cm) long, were not cast until the discovery that combining copper with tin produces bronze: an alloy hard enough to maintain a sharp cutting edge in combat. Bronze also kept a burnished gleam, resembling gold, further enhancing its desirability.

The art of making bronze alloys was developed around 3000 BCE in West Asia, marking the beginning of the Bronze Age. Bronze was easier to cast and strong enough to work into complex shapes, as well as taking a keener edge. Bronze workers discovered that metal becomes harder when beaten. They perfected the art of beating the bronze sword while it was cold and then tempering it to remove the brittleness. Metals derive their strength from the ability of metal atoms to form many bonds and thus link up with multiple neighbors. When they do this in an orderly way they create lattices of atoms, and the number and regularity of the bonds make these lattices hard to disrupt. Fracturing such a lattice depends on breaking a series of bonds and then re-forming them as the atoms realign — breaking a whole row of such bonds at once takes a lot of energy. But when there are flaws in the lattice, known as dislocations, it becomes possible to fracture the lattice by rearranging just a few atoms, which is much easier — in other words, the metal is weaker and more prone to breaking.

One way to overcome this is to beat the metal while it is cold, known as cold working or work hardening. The repeated hammering moves dislocations to the boundaries of the lattice, where they weaken the metal far less. This is why cold working bronze or iron makes for better blades.

Bronze swords spread across Eurasia over the next 1,500 years. The precise percentage of tin used to make the alloy affects the properties of a blade. More tin produces bronze that is harder but more brittle; less tin produces bronze that is softer but less likely to shatter in battle, and more likely instead to bend. The popularity

Bronze Age smiths casting swords in a prehistoric foundry.

of the leaf-blade design for Bronze Age swords is probably because it minimizes bending.

Bronze Age swords were typically made with a single casting for the blade and hilt. Fullers (long grooves) might be cut into the blade to lighten it and also to encourage the flow of blood from wounds. Blades were cast with broad shoulders to help guard the grip hand.

The Iron Age

By the end of the Bronze Age, bronze swords had edges almost as hard as steel, and superior to iron. However, bronze was expensive because tin is relatively rare; for instance, only being found in Europe in a few locations such as southwest Britain. As metalworking developed and higher temperatures could be achieved for smelting, so it became possible to produce workable iron. Iron ore is plentiful, so iron swords were cheaper and more widely available than bronze ones. Iron could also be used to make steel (albeit haphazardly for millennia), which could produce blades much harder and

sharper than bronze. With the advent of the Iron Age, around the 13th century BCE, iron swords began to displace bronze ones.

But copper and bronze weapons, and swords in particular, had already changed history. The development of copper and bronze weapon-casting created a class of skilled metalworking artisans, fostering long-range trading connections (such as the Phoenicians traveling to Cornwall in England for the tin trade) and cultural interchange. These in turn are credited with stimulating the development of urban civilizations, not to mention giving "civilized" peoples a decisive military advantage over Stone Age lifestyle "barbarians"; all this helps to account for the rise of the "great powers" of the Bronze Age (e.g. Egypt, Sumer, the Hittites, Mycenae, and so on).

06

Inventor(s):

Steppe peoples of southern Central Asia

HORSE AND WAR CHARIOT

Social

Political

Tactical

Technical

Type:

Mobile launch platform

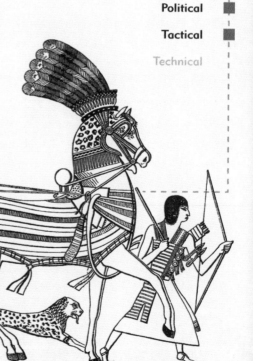

c. 2000 BCE

In military terms, the impact of the domestication of the horse was enormous, profound, and lasting. The horse became an integral and often dominant element of warfare up until the late 19th century (and continued to play important military roles up to and throughout the First World War). Horses could serve as weapons themselves, through sheer bulk and ferocity, but more importantly they served as a highly mobile platform for mounted warriors to access tactically important parts of the battlefield, and from which to launch lethal attacks. The nature of the military role of the domestic horse changed in ways that followed its evolution.

Breaking in

The precise date and location of the domestication of the horse have been contentious issues. In 2012 a DNA study by researchers at Cambridge University found that the horse was domesticated 6,000 years ago in the west Eurasian steppe, but that domestic horses were subsequently often bred with wild mares as they spread across Eurasia (mares provide the mitochondrial DNA for their foals).

Such an early date for domestication may be surprising to military historians, for it is not until the Sintashta burials and other early second millennium BCE archaeological sites that evidence appears of horses making an impact in military terms. It seems that for around 4,000

years horses were bred for purely agricultural purposes (for milk and meat). These early domestic horses were weak and small compared to modern ones, and not strong enough to pull loads, let alone to be ridden. In the third millennium BCE there is some evidence for the first wheeled carts, and the Sumerians eventually adapted these for war. The Battle Standard of Ur, a wood and mosaic artifact dating from c. 2500 BCE, shows scenes of Sumerian armies, including four-wheeled carts pulled by donkeys, carrying javelin-wielding men. But these donkey-carts were not the game-changers that would cement the equine role in warfare, offering low speed and poor maneuverability (with four wheels rather than just two, they would have been hard to turn from a straight line). Sometime around 2,000 BCE, however, this was to change, and the world would change in turn.

Chariotocracies

At the start of the second millennium BCE, horse breeders in the Eurasian steppes succeeded in producing a stronger animal.

" ... it is the lean steed that will prove of service, and not the fatted ox, on the day of battle."

SA'DI (1184–1292), *THE GULISTAN*, C. 1256 CE

Detail from the Standard of Ur, showing a four-wheeled chariot equipped with a quiver of javelins.

This was squarely in the middle of the Bronze Age, the period when metallurgy and smithing had reached a high degree of sophistication. The combination of enhanced horse power and technology resulted in a new weapon of war, the war chariot, which swept across Eurasia in the space of the next few centuries. The vehicle developed by these Bronze Age warriors was a light and nimble two-wheeled chariot, which could be handled with great skill to combine high speed (up to 24 mph/39 kph) with great maneuverability. The chariot typically had a two- or three-man crew, with one man driving the chariot and the other(s) launching weapons.

The impact of the chariot has been likened to that of the first tanks, offering a similar combination of mobility and armor. Charioteers could access all parts of the battlefield quickly to deliver rapid tactical responses. They could break enemy lines with terrifying charges, but also withdraw quickly when necessary.

The expense of the chariot system, involving high-quality horses and metalwork, implied an associated socio-economic system. Only the richest and most powerful strata of society could command the necessary resources; heavily armed and armored as a result, they were able to perpetuate their dominance through force of arms. Lowly foot soldiers, too poor to afford expensive bronze armor, were easy prey for the chariot-aristocracies — or chariotocracies — that rapidly came to dominate society. Waves of chariot-borne invaders spread the chariot meme from the steppes of southern Central Asia outward.

Around 1400 BCE technological advances changed the socio-economic equation and overturned the dominance of the chariotocrats. Iron had been worked since the mid-third millennium but around this time the discovery of carburization — hammering heated wrought iron to produce a steel edge/face — inaugurated the Iron Age in earnest. Iron is superior to bronze for arms and armor, but also, crucially, much more widely available. Metal gear was no longer the preserve of the elite, and the charioteers had to settle for a place in the ranks, alongside infantry armed and armored with steel. Chariots were useful, but the full military potential of the horse had yet to be tapped.

Here comes the cavalry

Around 900 BCE, horse breeders in south Central Asia succeeded in producing a bigger horse with a strong enough back to bear an armed man. Cavalry was born. In the absence of the stirrup (see page 44) and with truly enormous war horses yet to be bred, this early cavalry was light — the rider wearing padded or scaled armor, and equipped with javelin, lance, or bow. For much of the classical period cavalry was less important than the heavy infantry of the Greek hoplites and Roman legionaries (see pages 14 and 40), although even during this period, when infantry dominated warfare, cavalry was the key to some notable victories. Alexander and his famous Companions — the mounted elite of the Macedonian army — achieved stunning victories through judicious use of cavalry shock tactics and lightning charges. At Gaugamela in 331 BCE, Alexander inflicted a crushing defeat on a vastly superior Persian force under Darius, by launching a cavalry charge at the crucial juncture in the battle. Having lured the Persians into breaking their lines through clever deployment and maneuver of his own forces, Alexander led a daring cavalry charge through the gap to assault Darius himself, winning the day and a vast empire in consequence.

At Cannae in 216 BCE, the cavalry again proved key. In this battle, the Romans far outnumbered Carthaginian general Hannibal's forces in infantry terms, but ceded superiority in both quality and quantity of cavalry. Hannibal's cavalry were able to drive off the Roman horse and circle around behind the legionaries, completing the lethal envelopment that led to an unprecedented bloodbath.

Hannibal's cavalry included a contingent of "heavy cavalry"; bigger, stronger horses carrying men in heavier armor. Not long after this, true heavy cavalry would appear in the Middle East. Around 100 BCE the Parthians learned to feed alfalfa to brood mares in winter to produce heavy war horses, able to bear the weight of both armor and heavily armored riders. The resulting heavy cavalry, known as cataphracts, helped secure Parthian lands from steppe marauders for several centuries and would eventually spread the heavy cavalry meme via Byzantium to Europe.

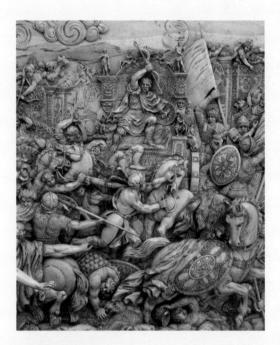

Alexander's cavalry charge turns the course of battle and the tide of history at the Battle of Gaugamela.

07

Inventor(s):

The ancient Assyrians

SIEGE
ENGINES

Type:

Siege weapons

Social

Political

Tactical ■

Technical ■

Second millennium BCE

In the Neolithic era, as people built permanent settlements and accumulated material wealth, so they began to fortify. By the start of the historical period some of these fortifications were astonishingly vast. Second-millennium Nineveh supposedly had stone walls 50 miles (80 km) long, 120 feet (37 m) high and 30 feet (9 m) thick, whereas its contemporary, Babylon, is known to have acquired immense walls. By the time of the Neo-Babylonian Empire (c. 600 BCE), Babylon was enclosed by huge walls, 12 miles (19 km) long, famously described by the ancient Greek Herodotus as wide enough on top for "a four-horse chariot to run."

Get higher

Overcoming such imposing fortifications meant engaging in lengthy, difficult, and costly sieges, with famine and disease as likely to destroy the besieging army as the defenders. Alternatively, the fortifications could be undermined, smashed through or overtopped, but getting, and staying, close enough to the walls of a fort or city to achieve these, under fire from arrows, rocks, and boiling oil, required some serious engineering. From around the second millennium BCE the Assyrian army developed into probably the first army in the world with different units serving specialized roles, and these included engineers. By the start of the first millennium at the latest they were building siege engines such as the six-wheeled siege tower with a central tower housing archers and a projecting battering ram shown in a relief from the palace of Nimrud, dating to the ninth century BCE.

Relief from first millennium BCE Nimrud showing a siege engine bearing a startling resemblance to a modern tank, where the "cannon" is a battering ram.

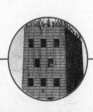

SIEGE ENGINES

The helepolis

The siege tower developed into a sophisticated and audacious feat of engineering under the ancient Greeks and Hellenes, reaching its apogee in the legendary *helepolis* of Epimachus. During the siege of Rhodes, Demetrius Poliorcetes, king of Macedon, called in "a famous Athenian architect named Epimachus," according to the Roman engineer and architect Vitruvius, who goes on to relate how Epimachus "constructed at enormous expense, with the utmost care and exertion, an *helepolis* one hundred and thirty-five feet [41 m] high and sixty feet [18 m] broad ... the machine itself weighed three hundred and sixty thousand pounds [163,293 kg]." The dimensions given by Vitruvius are probably inaccurate. Other ancient authors describe a pyramidal tower 130 feet (40 m) high, resting on eight wheels, with two internal staircases: one for going up and one for down.

According to the ancient historian Diodorus, it took 3,400 men to move this behemoth, although the actual method of propulsion is the topic of much debate. Diodorus suggests that the men pushed on heavy crossbeams at the bottom of the device, but there would not have been space for more than 800 of them. One suggestion is that the tower was rigged with pulleys and block and tackle, fixed to anchor points in front of the tower (or at least ahead of its rear axle). This would then have allowed more men and teams of oxen to work behind the tower, protected from enemy fire, pulling in the opposite direction to the motion of the tower. Diodorus even claims that "Besides wheels it had casters, so as to admit of being moved laterally as well as directly." The extraordinary labor and cost of the construction seems to have been wasted because Rhodes did not fall to the siege of Demetrius and he was forced to make terms with the inhabitants.

Towers and testudo

The Romans, typically, adopted this Hellenic military technology and refined it. They became expert at the construction and deployment of siege engines for use against enemy strongholds. Towers were clad in rawhide and layers of rags and daubed with noncombustible substances to protect against missiles and fire. During the Jewish Wars of the first century CE the Romans apparently took to cladding their siege towers with iron plates for further protection, although

"If army commanders carefully complete with logic and continuous diligence these siege machines, which have been selectively compiled for description and illustration, and always contemplate divine justice ... they will easily capture cities, especially those of Afar and themselves suffer nothing fatal from the God-damned enemy."

HERON OF BYZANTIUM, *PARANGELMATA POLIORCETICA* (*INSTRUCTIONS FOR SIEGE WARFARE*); C. 950 CE

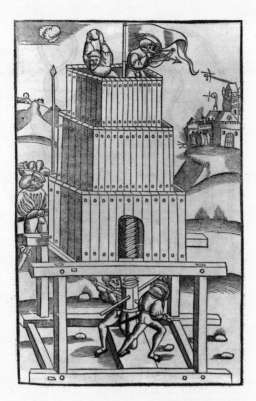

A telescoping siege engine from a 16th-century manuscript, where the tower is elevated by turning a screw at the base — probably not a real device.

the remains of a collapsed tower found at Jerusalem suggest that they did not always make structural compensations for the added weight.

Upper stories of a tower might be equipped with a drawbridge (known as a *pons* or *sambuca*) that could be dropped down on top of the wall to allow invading soldiers to stream out of the tower. Lower down might be a ram — a massive beam or entire tree trunk with an iron head in the shape of a ram. This was supplemented with specialized auxiliary devices to widen a breach once opened, such as a beam with an iron hook that could be pushed into a hole to drag out more stones, and the *terebus*, a smaller iron

point for dislodging individual stones. Rams might also travel with a single-story protective structure known as a *testudo* (tortoise).

Earth workers

By the fourth century Roman legions had one siege engine for every hundred legionaries; compare this to the ratio of three pieces of artillery for every thousand soldiers in a Napoleonic army. However, it should be noted that siege engines, for all their ingenuity and abundance, were probably less important to the efficacy of Roman siegecraft than the spade. Roman soldiers were expected to carry out the process of *castramentatio*, in which a camp with earthen ramparts, a ditch, and a wooden palisade was constructed every single night if they did not reach a permanent camp. They could achieve this in just three to four hours. Some feats of legionary spade work have become legendary. At the siege of Carthage in the mid-second century BCE, 6,000 men labored on a single earthwork built to support a giant battering ram. Battling the slave rebellion of Spartacus, Crassus had his troops dig a trench 15 feet deep, 15 feet wide (4.6 x 4.6 m) and 34 miles (55 km) long, across the toe of Italy. At the Siege of Alesia in 52 BCE, Caesar's legions shifted 70.5 cubic feet (2 million m³) of earth in constructing a system of trenches and earthworks (known as *circumvallations* and *contravallations*) that defeated Vercingetorix and protected the besieging Roman army from a relief force said to outnumber it five to one.

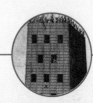

08

Inventor(s):
The ancient Greeks

BALLISTA

Type:
Artillery

Social

Political

Tactical ■

Technical ■

c. 300 BCE

A Roman legion came to the fray armed with more than just manpower and simple but effective tactics. They could also bring to bear a savagely destructive array of artillery devices, flinging huge iron-tipped bolts and heavy stones at terrifying speed, blasting holes in city walls, or picking out individual soldiers with armor-piercing precision.

Greek origins

From the Greek word meaning "to throw," the ballista is an ancient artillery weapon similar in basic plan to a large crossbow, though operating on slightly different principles. The first ballistae were built by the ancient Greeks and may indeed have been giant crossbows, using the principle of tension with thick wooden arms that bent as the bowstring was pulled back. When the bowstring was released, the arms sprang back into position, drawing the string forward and accelerating a bolt (i.e., large arrow) or stone to lethal velocity. Such devices were used with great success during the wars between Dionysius of Syracuse and Carthage in the fourth century BCE in Sicily; they had the power to fling fiery bolts into besieged towns and even to knock down walls.

Torsion power

Roman ballistae worked on a different principle to these early Greek ones, although this too was a Greek invention, encountered by the Romans during their clashes with Greek colonies during the Punic Wars of the third century BCE. This principle was torsion, in which energy is stored through twisting a resistant, elastic material, and released when it unwinds. In this case the material was animal sinew, wound into a thick skein of cords and able to store tremendous amounts of energy. Torsion was the power behind many forms of Roman artillery, including the onager and other catapults.

The basic design of a Roman ballista involved two bow arms, each one planted into a twisted skein of cords of sinew. The bowstring was pulled back by a lever and held in place by a ratchet. A bolt was then fitted into a groove, or a stone was inserted. Writing around 70 CE, the ancient Hellenic mathematician and mechanic Heron of Alexandria described the basic operating steps: "Thus, when the half-springs are strung and the arm recoils outward ... you must pull back the bowstring as described, load the missile, and squeeze the trigger." There is some controversy over whether ballistae were outswinging or inswinging; which is to say, whether the bow arms projected out from the skeins to give a crossbowlike appearance, or inward. Mainstream opinion is the former but

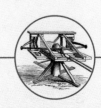

"Then heads were shattered, as masses of stone, hurled from the scorpions [small ballistae], crushed many of the enemy."

AMMIANUS MARCELLINUS, *RES GESTAE, BOOK XIX*, DESCRIBING THE SIEGE OF AMIDA IN 359

there is evidence for the latter, including the remains of the first attested preserved part of a true ballista, which were discovered at Hatra (Iraq) in 1972.

Around this basic plan was arrayed a complex frame of wood and metal, with devices for twisting the skeins to ratchet up the tension and other devices, such as winches, windlasses, or pulleys, to operate the bowstring lever. Roman ballistae were powerful and accurate. A typical ballista could shoot a 2.5-pound (1 kg) bolt over 300 yards (274 m), whereas a large one could hurl a 10-pound (4.5 kg) bolt over 450 yards (411 m).

They were so accurate that individuals could be targeted at a distance. This is attested to both by archaeological finds (such as the skeleton of an ancient Briton killed in battle with the Romans at Maiden Castle in 43 CE, found with a ballista bolt buried in his spine) and also by historical records. A classic example comes from Julius Caesar's own account of the invasion of Gaul. During the siege of Avaricum (Bourges) in 52 BCE the Romans were constructing a high siege terrace, which was about to overtop the defender's walls. Caesar writes that "They felt that the fate of Gaul depended entirely on what happened at that moment, and performed before our eyes an exploit so memorable that I felt I must not leave it unrecorded." He goes on to relate that, opposite one of the siege towers, a Gaul appeared, hurling pitch and tallow onto a fire that had been set in an attempt to destroy the terrace. The Romans targeted him with a ballista and killed him with a bolt, whereupon another man took his place and was shot in turn. This continued throughout the night. The tale is told as an illustration of the desperate heroism of the doomed Gauls, but serves equally well to drive home the impressive accuracy of the Roman ballistae.

A list of ballistae

The Romans adapted the basic ballista to produce a range of weapons. The most common was the *scorpio* (scorpion), a small, two-man-operated ballista that fired bolts like large arrows or stones weighing 4 Roman pounds (1.3 kg). When mounted on a cart or fitted with wheels to create mobile artillery, the scorpio was known as the *carroballista*, while the *cheiro-* and *manuballista* were small enough to be handheld, although probably still requiring a stand, a frame, and some sort of winch to load. Ballistae could be loaded with different types of bolt for different effects, in a similar fashion to the way that later artillery was equipped with different types of shot.

In the Republican and early imperial period the Roman ballista was constructed from hardened wood with iron plating. By the start of the second century CE, however, it had been redesigned and heavily engineered to produce an all-metal framework offering greater reliability and durability, more power and, crucially, an unobstructed view of the target. Some parts from these machines have survived in the archaeological record, and there are written descriptions of the all-metal *manuballista*.

Artillery service

In fact, through their adaptations and mutations of the original Greek model, the Romans had devised an entirely new arm of the military — a full-fledged tactical artillery service, offering options ranging from heavy siege weapons to mobile battlefield weapons that could travel with and support infantry units. With their panoply of ballistae the Romans anticipated modern artillery tactics, from heavy bombardment to suppressing fire. For instance, each legion would take up to 60 *scorpiones* into battle, setting them up in batteries on higher ground, just like artillery in the Napoleonic Wars. The *scorpiones* of one legion could lay down a sustained fire of up to 240 bolts per minute, achieving high levels of accuracy at ranges from 109 to 437 yards (100–400 m).

BALLISTA

09

Inventor(s):

The ancient Iberians

GLADIUS

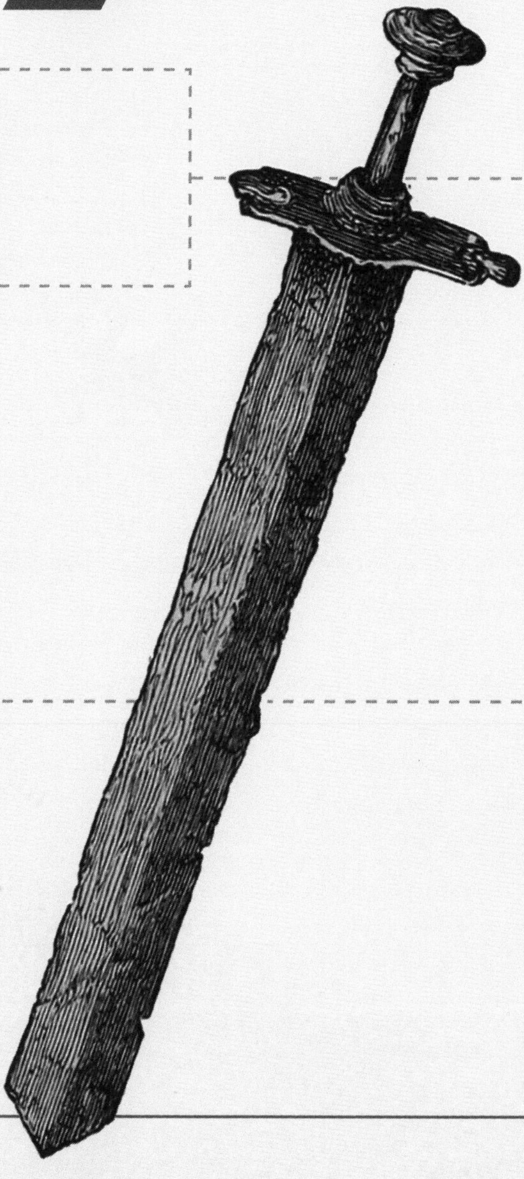

Type:
Stabbing weapon

Social

Political

Tactical

Technical

c. 200 BCE

The gladius has been called the "sword that had conquered the world"; as the primary killing tool of the Roman legionary, it was probably responsible for more deaths than any other sword in the ancient world. In fact, the gladius was not a single, unchanging weapon; its form evolved over the course of Roman history. In general, however, it can be described as a relatively light, wide, and short-bladed sword primarily designed for stabbing and thrusting.

Spanish steel

The gladius first gained popularity as the weapon of choice for Roman soldiers around 200 BCE, when it was known as the *gladius Hispaniensis* (Iberian sword), in reference to its supposed origins. Allegedly the Romans encountered it while battling with Iberian troops in the Punic Wars and were so impressed that they adopted it for themselves. The *gladius Hispaniensis* had a blade that was broad at the base and either ran largely parallel but with a long point, or tapered all the way to give an elongated pyramidal shape. The length of the blade was 25 to 27 inches (64–69 cm) and the width 1.5 to 2 inches (4–5 cm).

The weight of the blade was balanced by a chunky round pommel, with a simple grip and hand guard of bone or wood. The large pommel also helped to keep the gladius from being wrenched or pulled from the bearer's hand when a pierced opponent recoiled or twisted. Ideal for penetrating light armor of the sort worn by enemies of Rome, the gladius was shorter than many swords wielded by the opposition, but its relative lightness and the economy of movement implied by thrusting rather than slashing meant that it could be wielded more efficiently. Legionaries would still have the energy to fight when their opponents were exhausted.

The ideal *gladius Hispaniensis* was forged from pure Iberian iron. Swordsmiths were reputed to test the flexibility of a freshly forged blade by resting it across their heads and pulling down the hilt and tip ends until they touched the shoulders. When released, a true blade would spring back to the level. The sword was contained in a scabbard that might be decorated with plates, perhaps of stamped tin or bronze.

The corroded remains of a first-century CE *gladius Hispaniensis*, showing how the blade, guard, tang, and pommel were cast as a single piece.

Cut or thrust?

The hallmark of the gladius was its versatility and the balance it offered between all the needs of the infantry man. All modern experts concur that it was not solely a thrusting weapon; with its double edges it could also lop off heads and limbs. Ancient authors, however, most definitely emphasized the thrusting aspect. In his late fourth-century *De Re Militari* (*On Military Matters*), Vegetius wrote that, "They [the legionaries] were likewise taught not to cut but to thrust with their swords."

Mainz to Pompeii

Around the time of Augustus (c. 1 CE), the *gladius Hispaniensis* began to be supplanted by an evolution of the design. This is known as the Mainz-type gladius, after the location at which the most famous example was discovered: the so-called Sword of Tiberius, now residing in the British Museum in London. Its richly decorated scabbard shows that it probably belonged to an officer. Mainz-type gladii have slightly shorter and stockier blades than Iberian ones, typically around 20 to 24 inches (50–60 cm) long and 2 to 2.4 inches (5–6 cm) wide, with a graceful waisted, leaf-shaped profile. A related form, found at Fulham in London, is similarly waisted but less graceful and more angular, perhaps reflecting a lack of smithing skill or simply a desire to adopt simpler and more efficient production methods.

Mainz/Fulham-type gladii were supplanted after a few decades by the Pompeian gladius, named after specimens recovered from the ruins of Pompeii. Said to have been inspired by the style of gladius used in the arena (for which the gladiator was named), the Pompeian gladius is still shorter at 16.5 to 21.6 inches (42–55 cm), weighing just over 2 pounds (1 kg). A lighter, shorter sword could be wielded faster. Pompeian gladii had parallel edges with a shorter pyramidal stabbing point than previous types.

The gladius was not the only sword used by the Roman army. Cavalry, striking from horseback, used a longer-bladed sword known as the *spatha*. As the Roman legionary system declined toward the end of the Western Roman Empire, and the armies of Rome came increasingly to be made up of "barbarian" auxiliaries and mercenaries, so the gladius fell out of favor. These non-Roman soldiers used their own style of weapons, which were more effective in the less disciplined battlefield tactics they employed, with less close-quarter fighting. By the third century CE the gladius had largely given way to the *spatha*.

" ... the Romans not only made a jest of those who fought with the edge of the sword, but always found them an easy conquest."

Flavius Vegetius Renatus, *De Re Militari* (I.12)

Mass weapon of destruction

With its simple outline and hilt and guard made from cheap organic materials, the gladius may not have been the acme of sword technology, but it was the perfect standard-issue weapon. Easy to mass-produce — an important consideration given that at any one time the Roman army would have had around 250,000 sets of equipment in service — it perfectly complemented the Roman way of fighting.

Roman tactics emphasized discipline and close-knit formations. Legionaries advanced in lines, throwing their pila (javelins) when in range, before drawing their gladii and closing as quickly as possible to hand-combat range.

Belt or baldric?

Most right-handed swordsmen find it easy to draw a sword from a scabbard worn on the left, but for legionaries to wear their gladii in this fashion would have endangered the man to the left. Statuary depictions of legionaries show that they wore the gladius on the right, either from a belt or a baldric (a strap slung over one shoulder). In the latter case, it is not clear how to draw the sword with one hand without the scabbard lifting up as well. Modern-day reenactors find that wearing a belt that passes through the baldric holds the scabbard in place, allowing for a single-handed draw (vital when the other hand clutches a shield).

Roman legionary holding a pilum and wearing a sheathed gladius on a baldric.

10

Inventor(s):

Southern Siberian
horsemen

STIRRUPS

Type:

Fighting platform

Social ■

Political ■

Tactical ■

Technical

c. First century BCE

Horses and cavalry had made a huge impact on warfare as far back as the Bronze Age (see page 28), yet in the West, during the classical period, the infantry was inexorably ascendant. The Romans relegated cavalry to the fringes of battle, often leaving it to their low-status auxiliary forces to run this part of the army. By the Middle Ages the picture had radically changed, with several centuries during which the mounted knight on horseback was seemingly dominant.

In the 19th century, the start of this reversal of fortunes between the infantry and cavalry was decisively dated to the Battle of Adrianople in 378 CE, where Roman legions were overwhelmed by the cavalry of the Goths. In a catastrophic defeat that the fourth-century CE Archbishop of Milan, St. Ambrose, called "the end of all humanity, the end of the world," some 40,000 Romans, including the Emperor Valens, were massacred when taken in the flanks by a force of heavy Ostrogoth cavalry. "Nor, except the Battle of Cannae, is so destructive a slaughter recorded in our annals," wrote the Roman historian Ammianus Marcellinus just a decade or so later.

The man on horseback

By the early 20th century a different view began to emerge. Although it may have been true that, after Adrianople, the Romans belatedly tried to bolster their own cavalry forces, it is clear that cavalry did not gain the ascendancy until much later. After the collapse of the Western Roman Empire, dominion over Europe passed into the hands of "barbarian" peoples, most notably the Franks. Under the Merovingian and later Carolingian dynasties, the Franks struggled to unify much of Europe under their banner while fighting off attacks from Saracens (Muslim invaders to the south), horse-riding peoples from the east, such as the Avars, and Viking sea raiders from the north and west. In the process the previous social order of the late Roman empire transitioned to feudalism, where power devolved in a pyramidal structure with local lords exercising ownership over a parcel of land and its inhabitants, in return for offering fealty to a higher noble. In return for this local power, the feudal lord was expected to provide upon demand a fully equipped fighting force spearheaded by mounted knights in armor. These knights were supposedly all-conquering, with battles viewed as essentially combats between men on horseback in which infantry were a despised low-status sideshow.

What was the catalyst for this extraordinary revolution in the social, political, economic, and military order of the day? According to Lynn White, in his seminal 1962 book *Medieval Technology and Social Change*, it was the stirrup,

STIRRUPS

45

a wood, rope, or metal tread or toehold at the end of a strap hanging from a saddle. The earliest stirrups date back to around the first century BCE, either from southern Siberia or India, depending on the source. By the fifth to sixth centuries CE it had spread east to China and Korea, and west as far as the Avar. Equipped with stirrups, the mounted warriors of the Avar were so effective that the author of the early seventh century Byzantine military manual the *Strategikon* claimed, somewhat credulously, "they have been brought up on horseback, and owing to their lack of exercise they simply cannot walk about on their own feet." According to White, however, the stirrup did not filter through into Europe until around the ninth century CE, but when it did arrive its effects were transformative.

The shock of the new

"Few inventions have been so simple as the stirrup, but few have had so catalytic an influence on history," wrote White, setting out his influential and controversial thesis connecting the "stirrup, mounted shock combat, feudalism, and chivalry." "The Man on Horseback, as we have known him during the past millennium, was made possible by the stirrup, which joined man and steed into a fighting organism." White argued that the stirrup made it possible for a mounted man to adopt a new and all-conquering fighting style — "mounted shock combat" — where the rider charged with a couched lance (i.e., one held underarm and against the body), able to ram into his target with unstoppable force yet withstand the shock and remain in the saddle. With the stirrup the heavy armored cavalry became the pre-eminent force in the land, but this had socio-economic ramifications. The cost of a heavy horse and heavy arms and armor was exorbitant, and could not be met by the centralized authority (i.e., the king and his court). Instead, the responsibility for outfitting and maintaining this new breed of soldier was devolved upon the rider himself, and he was given the lands and subjects necessary to fund it. Feudalism was the inevitable consequence of the adoption of the stirrup and became a self-perpetuating system: "The requirements of the new mode of warfare which it made possible," wrote White, "found expression in a new form of Western European society dominated by an aristocracy of warriors endowed with land so that they might fight in a new and highly specialized way."

"Then the Count of Saint-Pol stood up on his stirrups, drew his sword, and distributed blows so great that he split and broke the press of his enemies with his marvellous virtue."

THE BATTLE OF BOUVINES ACCORDING TO WILLIAM THE BRETON, 1214

The Stirrup Controversy

This thesis of technological determinism came in for crushing criticism. One of its most vigorous critics, Bernard Bachrach, argued that the archaeological evidence did not show "that the use of the stirrup was common among horsemen or that it helped bring about the development of mounted shock combat." He claimed that the stirrup did not become militarily important for at least two centuries after its introduction to Western Europe. Writing on what he calls "The Stirrup Controversy," Professor John Sloan notes that White "focuses on the technological question without considering the more fundamental issue of the relationship of military institutions (army structures) to the social-political institutions of the societies that create them."

Other criticisms leveled at White's theory include the likelihood that the Avars introduced the stirrup and the "shock combat" fighting style to Europe long before the advent of feudalism; the role of the saddle as the crucial element enabling couched-lance charges; and the use of stirrup-enabled heavy cavalry by many other states and peoples — such as the Byzantines and Arabs — who did not fall into feudalism as a result.

Today the stirrup is recognized as an important element in the development of heavy cavalry and associated fighting styles, but it is seen as simplistic to argue for a one-way causal sequence flowing from adoption of the stirrup to heavy cavalry with shock-combat tactics to the feudal state. As far back as 1924 Sir Charles Oman, the doyen of military historians, noted in his *A History of the Art of War in the Middle Ages* that "the tendency [of the Merovingian and Carolingian Franks] (to shift from general levy to retainers) was all the easier because a well-armed band of henchmen, however small, some or all of them mounted, was worth a much larger count's general levy." In other words, the declining state of internal security was a primary driver in the development of feudal cavalry systems.

The controversy over the role and impact of the stirrup is illustrative of a wider debate over the importance of technology as a determining factor in military history. John Sloan asks: "can anyone imagine that, if Caesar with his legions had found the army of Charlemagne, Fulk the Black, or William the Conqueror arrayed for battle in northern Gaul, he would not have destroyed it at least as fast as the Romans overcame the Celts, stirrups notwithstanding?" In other words, the socio-economic edifice behind the military is the major determinant: the legions of an organized, coherent, well-ordered, and economically powerful state will always overcome the army of a socio-economically chaotic polity, no matter how well armed and mounted their troops. Ultimately, socio-economics trumps technology.

11

GREEK
FIRE

Type:

Flammable liquid

Social

Political ■

Tactical

Technical ■

c. 678 CE

Greek fire is one of the great mysteries of military history — a terrifying weapon that changed the course of history, the secret of which is now lost. Often likened to modern-day napalm, it was a flammable mixture of exotic substances that clung to its targets and was almost impossible to extinguish, spreading fear and chaos.

Light my fire

Greek fire and related terms such as Persian or liquid fire were applied to a variety of flammable weapons in the Middle Ages, but true Greek fire was the secret recipe belonging to the Byzantines, apparently formulated in the late seventh century. Its antecedents, however, stretch back to ancient times. Some form of liquid fire appears to be represented in Assyrian bas-reliefs, whereas other relatively simple incendiary devices such as pots of boiling oil and flaming naphtha (the ancient term for naturally occurring pitch/petroleum) were in use at least as far back as Biblical times, and were known to, and used by, the Greeks and Romans.

The Byzantines themselves seem to have used a precursor to Greek fire on at least one occasion, as attested by an account in the Chronicle of John Malalas, dating to c. 570 CE. He relates how the emperor Anastasios, struggling to put down a rebellion by a Thracian general named Vitalian in 516 CE, called for the help of "the philosopher Proclus of Athens, a famous man." Proclus advised the imperial counselor Marinus the Syrian:

"Take what I give you and go out against Vitalian." And the philosopher ordered that a large amount of what is known as elemental sulphur be brought in and that it be ground into fine powder. He gave it to Marinus with the words, "Wherever you throw some of this, be it at a building or a ship, after sunrise, the building or ship will immediately ignite and be destroyed by fire" … Vitalian set out to attack Constantinople, confident that he would certainly capture it and crush Marinus, who was coming to meet him, together with the force under his command. Marinus distributed the elemental sulphur … telling the soldiers and sailors, "There is no need for weapons but throw some of this at the ships that are coming against you and they will burn …" […] all the ships of the rebel Vitalian caught fire and were set ablaze and plunged to the bottom of the Bosphorus, taking with them the Gothic, Hunnish, and Scythian soldiers who had joined him.

> "Greek fire … What could be more dangerous in a conflict at sea? What could be more savage?"

THE CHRONICLE OF THE THIRD CRUSADE: THE ITINERARIUM PEREGRINORUM ET GESTA REGIS RICARDI, C. 1190; EDITED AND TRANSLATED BY HELEN J. NICHOLSON

A hand siphon — a handheld Greek fire dispenser — in action from a flying bridge during a siege, shown in a Byzantine *poliorcetica*, or manual of siege warfare.

Smells like victory

A century and a half later the Byzantine Empire faced its greatest threat — the Arab expansion in the early years of Islam. The conquests of the Ummayad caliphate had brought them almost to the gates of Constantinople, but the mighty fortifications could not be overcome while the Empire still controlled the seas. Between 672 and 678 CE Ummayad armies and fleets besieged Constantinople, but by land and sea they were confronted with a new secret weapon, supposedly developed for the emperor Constantine Pogonatus by a Christian Syrian refugee, Kallinikos of Heliopolis.

The actual mixture was only half the story, however — a key element was the technology developed for spraying Greek fire. Constantine had his *dromons* (war galleys) fitted with *siphons*, the name given to a pump-powered dispenser. It probably consisted of a container in which the Greek fire mixture could be heated, before being pumped out of the mouth of a tube held between the jaws of a bronze dragon or lion, suspended in front of which was an igniter. Thus, Greek fire was actually a sophisticated flame-throwing weapon system. It proved devastating both to the Arab fleet and to soldiers on land, where it was dispensed by the defenders from *cheirosiphons*, handheld versions of the naval siphons.

Partly thanks to Greek fire, the Arabs were forced to call off the siege in 678, and another siege met with a similar fate in 717. The successful defense of Constantinople is widely credited as one of the most important battles in world history. At the time much of Europe consisted of weak and chaotic polities that might have been easy prey to Muslim invaders (as in North Africa and Spain). Byzantium was the only organized state left in the Mediterranean; if it had fallen, the path through the Balkans and into Central Europe would have been clear for Arab armies. As it was, Constantinople held out for another 750 years, giving Europe a vital breathing space to develop strong nation states capable of defending themselves.

The secret formula

The precise recipe was always a closely guarded secret, now lost, but it is generally assumed to have been a mixture of sulfur, pitch, niter, petroleum, and quicklime. It may even have contained magnesium (a constituent of modern incendiary weapons). Magnesium is a highly reactive metal that will even burn underwater, one of the characteristics attributed to Greek fire, which helped to make it such a fearsome weapon.

The fire goes out

Greek fire was considered a state secret. Writing to his son in the mid-10th century, Emperor Constantine VII Porphyrogenitus stressed that the secret must not be revealed even to allies. Perhaps as a result of this secrecy the recipe was lost, and by 1204 it seems that the package of technologies that made it such a potent weapon was no longer available to the Byzantines.

However, similar incendiary weapons were already in use by the Saracens by this time, and were deployed against the Crusaders. Written around 1190, the *Itinerarium Peregrinorum et Gesta Regis Ricardi*, a chronicle of the Third Crusade, describes how the Saracens at Damietta were engulfed in their own flames when the wind changed, and gave helpful advice about how to extinguish it:

> It cannot be extinguished with water; but it can be put out by shaking sand over it. Pouring vinegar over it brings it under control.

Jean de Joinville, in his chronicle of the Seventh Crusade, describes the use of Greek fire by the Saracens at the battle of Al Mansurah in 1250, where missiles loaded with it were fired from great ballistae and looked, he wrote,

> [L]ike a big tun, and had a tail the length of a large spear; the noise which it made resembled thunder, and it appeared like a great fiery dragon flying through the air, giving such a light that we could see in our camp as clearly as in broad day.

With the introduction of gunpowder, however, and particularly the fitting out of warships with cannons, Greek fire became obsolete because ships could not get within range to deploy it.

Medieval trebuchet flinging a barrel of "Greek fire" (i.e., flammable substance) into a besieged stronghold.

12

Inventor(s):
European swordsmiths

MEDIEVAL SWORD

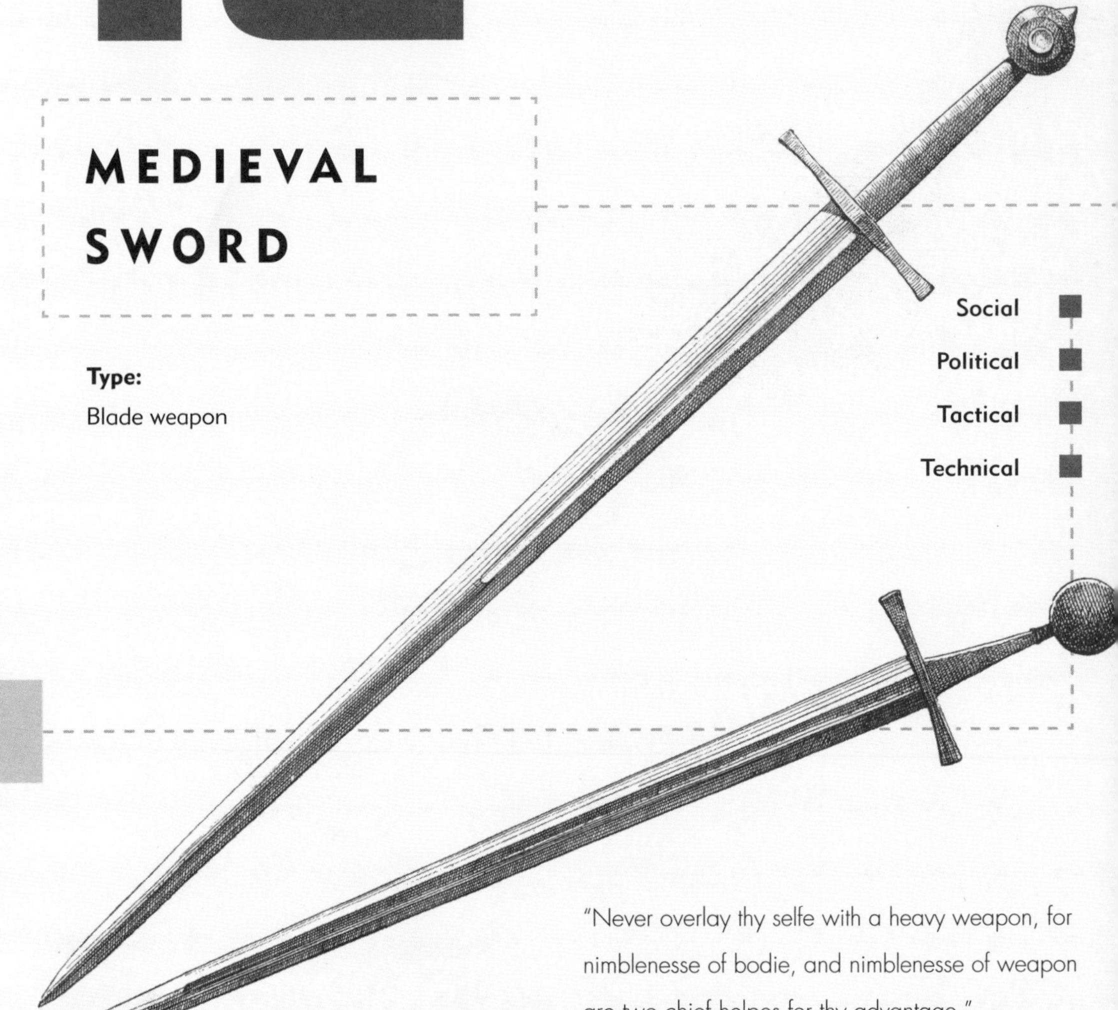

Type:

Blade weapon

Social ■

Political ■

Tactical ■

Technical ■

"Never overlay thy selfe with a heavy weapon, for nimblenesse of bodie, and nimblenesse of weapon are two chief helpes for thy advantage."

JOSEPH SWETNAM, *THE SCHOOLE OF THE NOBLE AND WORTHY SCIENCE OF DEFENCE* (1617)

1000–1600 CE

During the medieval period a bewildering variety of swords were employed in Europe, from the one-handed swords of the Vikings to the *Zweihänder* of the 16th-century Swiss *Doppelsöldner,* which could be up to 6 feet (1.8 m) long. The quintessential European sword of this era was the longsword, a straight double-edged blade over 35 inches (89 cm) long, weighing 2 to 4.5 pounds (0.9–2 kg), which could be wielded with one or two hands, or even with a "hand-and-a-half" grip.

Arming swords

The longsword (German: *langes Schwert*, Italian: *spadone*) developed from the more ubiquitous arming sword, a generic name for the sword a knight wore on his belt. The arming sword was a relatively short one-handed blade, designed to cut through chain mail, while also allowing the bearer to hold a shield, typically a small, round one known as a buckler.

The arming sword derived in turn from similar swords used by the Vikings and Normans. The arming sword would typically have a simple cross-guard (also known as a cruciform hilt), and a wide, fairly thin blade, with chisel-like edges and a flattened or hollow hexagonal cross section.

Arming swords dominated from around 1000 to 1350, but swords were part of a complex tapestry of arms and armor. To cope with the effect of crossbows, longbows, and pole-arms, armor was changing, with plate mail increasingly replacing chain mail. By the late 15th century a knight might be covered in articulated plate mail with no apparent chinks in his armor. This in turn fed into the design of swords. The arming sword morphed into a longer, slightly heavier weapon (although it is a common myth that the longsword was unwieldy and heavy), which remained versatile but was increasingly designed for piercing.

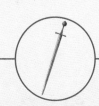

The art of fighting

The aim of the longsword wielder was to thrust the point of the sword into gaps between plates, possibly after having opened these by bashing, denting, or prying. Use of the longsword developed into a complex and sophisticated martial art, such as the *Kunst des Fechtens* (The Art of Fighting) of the 14th-century German fencing master Johannes Liechtenauer. Although Liechtenauer encrypted his instructions in a series of coded verses to keep them secret, his students passed on and developed his system, resulting in a well-recorded tradition.

The core of the longsword martial art lay in the four guards — defensive/offensive starting positions for all moves. These were known as the Plough (*Pflug*), the Ox (*Ochs*), the Roof (*Vom Tag*, literally "from the roof"), and the Fool (*Alber*). For instance, the Fool guard involves holding the sword with its point nearly on the ground, thus inviting the opponent to attack. In the Plough guard the sword is held with the hilt at the waist and the blade pointed at the opponent's eyes. From these guards the longsword fencer could segue into either defensive parries, or attacking moves. In the Liechtenauer tradition the latter included the *Drei Wünder* (Three Wounders): the strike, the thrust, and the slice.

All parts of the sword were used; for instance, the cross-guard could be used to catch an opponent's blade and drag him closer or push him off-balance. The fencer might put the pommel in the palm of the hand to get more thrust; he might even grab his own blade about halfway up its length, a technique known as *Halbschwert* (half-sword) that gave more control for disarming twists.

Two of the basic guards of longsword combat shown in an illustration from a 15th-century *Fechtbuch* (fight book or martial-arts manual).

A sword by any other name

The terminology of medieval and early Renaissance swords is complex and often confusing, particularly since many of the most common names are actually later interpolations. For instance, the term "broadsword" is now commonly used to refer to all medieval swords, but was never used historically. It was an 18th/19th-century invention, coined to differentiate the relatively wide blades of medieval swords (used for slashing and hacking as well as stabbing and thrusting) from later, narrower swords. Similarly, the term *Zweihänder* (two-hander) is a relatively modern term for swords that might have been known as *Doppelhänder* (double-hander) or *Bidenhänder* (both-hander), slaughter-swords, or *Schlachterschwerter* (battle swords).

Greatswords

The 16th and 17th centuries saw the last flowering of the sword for the man on foot on the battlefield (swords would continue to be important for cavalrymen and duelists up to the end of the 19th century). The longsword evolved into a true giant, variously known as the greatsword, double-hander, or true two-handed sword. This was a blade of prodigious length that required both hands to wield, and even had a secondary grip above the cross-guard, known as the *ricasso*. This was a blunt-edged stretch of the blade, and was itself guarded by projections, sometimes known as *Parrierhaken* (parrying hooks).

Possibly the original impetus for the two-handed sword was to produce a sword heavy enough to do serious damage to plate armor, but in practice cutting through such armor was impossible, and greatswords are,

cross-hilt sword, say, and 7 to 8 pounds [3–4 kg] for a Landsknecht two-handed sword, to give just a couple of examples from weapons in this collection. Processional two-handed swords are usually heavier, true, but rarely more than 10 pounds [4.5 kg]."

Keeping the sword light was a matter of simple physics, because the equation for kinetic energy (the energy a sword blade builds up and which it uses to generate impact force) is ½ x mass x velocity². A lighter sword is faster, and the equation shows that whereas doubling the mass of a blade can double the impact force, doubling its velocity provides four times as much energy.

Nonetheless, effectively wielding a blade that could be up to 6 feet (1.8 m) long required both skill and great strength. The Swiss/German *Dopplehänder* was used by the biggest soldiers, who were known as *Doppelsoldners* and received double pay. Their primary purpose was not single combat with knights (although amazingly they were sometimes used in duels), but breaking up pike squares by knocking aside and even cutting off the ends of pikes and halberds, before slashing and stabbing their wielders. For instance, in the early 1500s the Italian humanist historian Paulus Jovius described Swiss soldiers using two-handed greatswords to chop the shafts of pikes at the battle of Fornovo in 1495.

Engraving of the Battle of Fornovo in 1495, showing pike squares that would have been the target of Swiss *Doppelsöldner* and their two-handed swords.

despite appearance and popular myth, not that heavy. David Edge, former head curator and current conservator of the Wallace Collection, a museum in London noted for its collection of arms and armor, explains: "Original weapons are indeed far lighter than most people realize … 3 pounds [1.4 kg] for an 'average' late-medieval

A Longsword

[A] Pommel
[B] Grip
[C] Cross-guard
[D] Hilt
[E] Strong half

[F] Short edge
[G] Long edge
[H] Weak half
[I] Point
[J] Blade

The hilt includes the pommel (large to act as a counterweight), the grip, and the cross-guard. The blade is divided into two halves; the lower half, closer to the guard, is known as the strong half; the upper half is the weak half. These terms refer to the leverage that can be applied when the blade is pressed against another. If contact is made with the tip, only weak leverage can be applied and the blade is easily pushed aside, but can also be maneuvered much more quickly. The blades of the sword are named according to how it is held: the "long" edge is the edge closest to the second knuckle on the grip; the short edge is the one closest to the forearm.

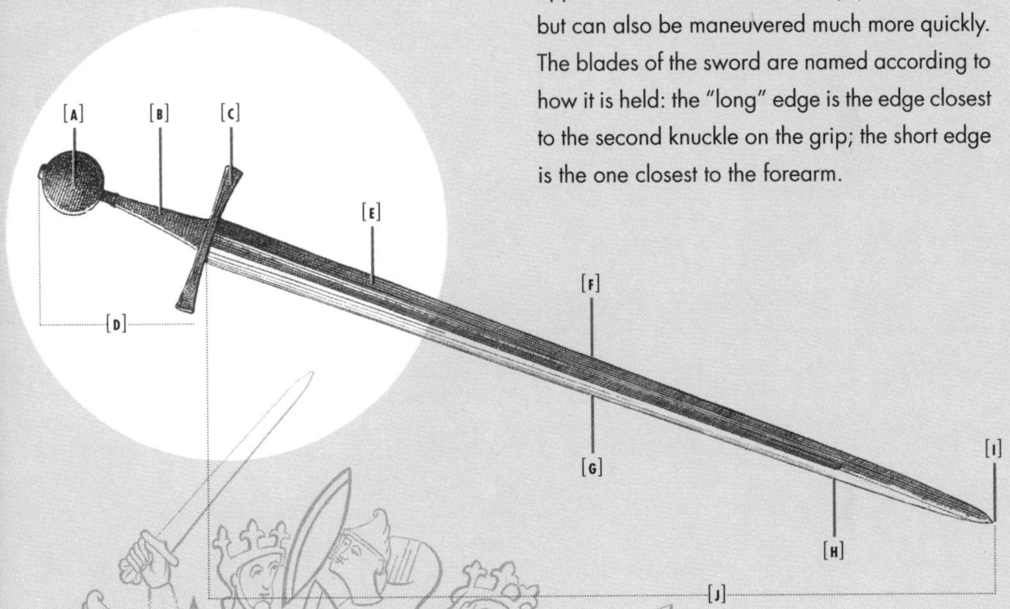

[A] [B] [C] [E] [F] [G] [H] [I] [J] [D]

KEY FEATURE:
THE EDGE

The cutting edge of the sword was its key offensive feature, but the edge was extremely vulnerable to notching and nicking, so it was important to parry blows where possible with the flat of the blade, or risk ending up with a blade "like a saw, toothed in great notches," in the words of 15th-century Spanish knight Don Pero Niño.

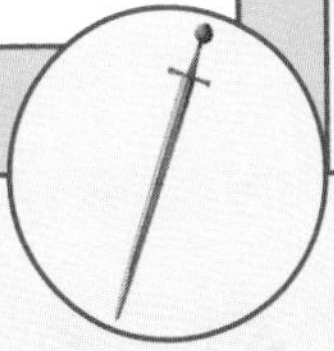

13

COUNTERWEIGHT TREBUCHET

Type:

Heavy artillery

Social

Political

Tactical

Technical

Before 1097

The trebuchet is a catapult that operates on a simple lever principle — when one end goes down, the other end goes up and hurls an attached projectile. Yet the simplicity of its conception disguises the engineering genius involved, the devastating effect of the weapon, and the far-reaching consequences attributed to its invention. Paul Chevedden, trebuchet historian, describes the device as "the high point in the development of mechanical warfare," whereas other historians have gone so far as to credit the trebuchet with a role in the emergence of the nation state, the development of clockwork, and innovations in theoretical mechanics.

Traction, hybrid, or counterweight

There are three types of trebuchet: traction, hybrid, and counterweight. All have a similar overall configuration, with a long arm mounted on a frame and pivoted near the base. The long section is either cupped to hold a stone or has a sling attached. In a traction trebuchet, man or animal power is used to pull down the short end; in a hybrid engine, a counterweight is added to the end of the short section to assist the pullers. A counterweight trebuchet operates through gravity. A heavy counterweight is lifted when the throwing arm is pulled down, and drops when the throwing arm is released. In its most developed form the counterweight consisted of a box that could be filled with earth or stones. The sketchbook of Villard de Honnecourt (c. 1230) shows a counterweight box with a volume of about 635 cubic feet (18 m³), which could hold up to 33.6 tons (30 tonnes) of ballast. Such a device could hurl a 220-pound (100 kg) stone over 437 yards (400 m) and a 551-pound (250 kg) stone over 175 yards (160 m). Stones up to 3,307 pounds (1,500 kg) could be launched by the biggest trebuchets.

The whirlwind and the ass

The word trebuchet comes from the Middle French verb *trebucher*, meaning "to tumble" or "to fall over," but the device itself has ancient Chinese origins and was in use by the fourth century BCE. The Chinese military treatise *Wu Jing Zong Yao* describes traction trebuchets from a small but rapid-firing two-man model to one named the Whirlwind, where a 250-man pulling crew was capable of throwing a 132-pound (60 kg) stone-shot over 82 yards (75 m). Traction trebuchets could achieve impressive rates of fire.

From the Chinese the technology passed via the Arabs to the Byzantines, and from them via a captured engineer named Bousas to the Avaro-Slavs who were encroaching into the Balkans. Hybrid trebuchets could throw heavier and farther. During the siege of Chandax (Heraklion) in 960–61 CE, a Byzantine trebuchet is said to have hurled a live ass, which may have weighed over 440 pounds (200 kg), over the city walls.

COUNTERWEIGHT TREBUCHET

The Daughter of the Earthquake

The development of the counterweight marked a step-change in trebuchet design. There is controversy over its origins, but it seems likely that it was invented before 1097, by the Byzantine emperor Alexios I Komnenos, who was outfitting the Franks of the First Crusade with the devices they would need to tackle mighty Saracen fortifications. His daughter, the chronicler Anna Komnene, recorded that at the siege of Nicaea in 1097, the emperor constructed large trebuchets that she called *helepolis* (city-takers — see page 34), which "were not fashioned according to conventional designs for such machines but followed ideas which he had devised himself and which amazed everyone."

The Crusaders must have spread this development across Europe. An eyewitness account of the Norman siege of Thessalonike in 1185 speaks of "newly invented heavy artillery," including a giant trebuchet named "The Daughter of the Earthquake." In 1199 a counterweight trebuchet, known as a *trabuchus*, was definitively recorded for the first time in Europe at the siege of Castelnuovo Bocca d'Adda in northern Italy. By the Second Crusade, immense trebuchets were in use that spread awe and fear.

Trebuchets combined a rapid rate of fire and great power with relatively inexpensive construction (although building a large engine could be a huge engineering project: it took 54 people three months to build "Warwolf," a giant trebuchet constructed for Edward I in his campaign against the Scots at the start of the 14th century). As a result they persisted as elements of the siege train until long after the siege cannon had made other pre-gunpowder siege engines obsolete.

A trebuchet in action at the Siege of Acre, during the Third Crusade.

"On the following day they again brought up these trebuchets covered with freshly skinned hides and planks, and placing them closer to the city walls, shooting, they hurled mountains and hills against us. For what else might one term these immensely large stones?"

JOHN I, ARCHBISHOP OF THESSALONIKE, *MIRACLES OF ST. DEMETRIUS*, C. 615

The Counterweight Trebuchet

[A] Swinging box counterweight
[B] Sling
[C] Throwing arm
[D] Frame

The counterweight trebuchet not only increased the power that could be generated to hurl stones, but also did away with the need for a pulling crew who took up the space beneath the throwing arm. Now there was space under the beam for a trough or runway in which the sling could run, which in turn made it possible to use a longer sling, giving a longer range.

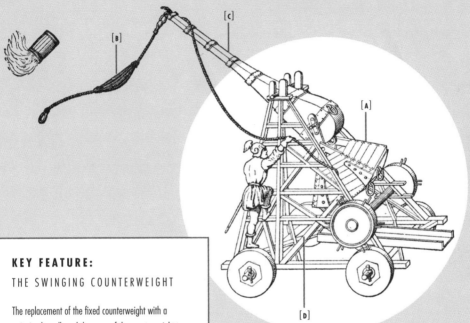

KEY FEATURE:
THE SWINGING COUNTERWEIGHT

The replacement of the fixed counterweight with a swinging box allowed the mass of the counterweight to be varied, in turn making it possible to alter the range of the trebuchet. Great feats of accuracy were possible. William of Tyre's account of the second Siege of Tyre in 1124 describes how an Armenian artillery expert named Havedic "displayed so much skill in directing the machines and hurling the great stone missiles that whatever was assigned to him as a target was at once destroyed without difficulty."

14

MEDIEVAL CROSSBOW

Type:

Projectile weapon

Social

Political

Tactical

Technical

"Hateful to God and unfit for Christians."
Pope Innocent II on the crossbow, 1139

c. 13th century

Although invented in China by around the sixth century BCE and known to the ancient Greeks and Romans in the form of early ballistae, the crossbow did not have its heyday until the late Middle Ages in Europe. Introduced to Europe around the 10th century, the crossbow offered power with ease of use and, initially, relative simplicity of construction. With a surface for the bolt to lie on, a nut to hold the spanned bowstring in place, and a trigger to release the string on demand, the crossbow made it possible to fire a powerful projectile in similar fashion to firing a latter-day firearm.

Draw and span

The physics of the bow mean that the efficiency of conversion of energy stored in the bow to energy imparted to the projectile depends on variables such as the mass of the string and the bolt. Crossbows had relatively heavy bolts, and in particular heavy strings (needed to cope with the enormous draw weight generated by the crossbow), and so were not particularly efficient at converting draw into bolt speed. The answer was to increase the draw weight still further through use of innovative materials for the bow, such as composite materials and later steel. These were able to generate devastatingly powerful draw weights, far in excess of the longbow. Early crossbows had draw weights of around 150 pounds (68 kg) and effective ranges not much more than 70 yards (64 m), but a 15th-century example spanned by a mechanical ratchet known as a *cranequin* had a draw weight of 397 pounds (180 kg), more than double that of the most powerful longbow. A large wall-mounted crossbow spanned by a windlass could command 1,200 pounds (544 kg), giving it a range of 459 yards (420 m).

Generating such powerful draws inevitably meant that spanning the crossbow was hard work. The ancient Greeks were said to have used "belly bows," where the bow was braced against the belly for spanning, possibly by the legs, with the archer lying down. Early medieval crossbows might be drawn by using a stirrup (i.e., toe or foot loop) on the end of the stock to allow the bowman to use his leg strength. This "claw" was soon supplemented by a belt loop to which the string could be attached — using the "belt and claw" system the bowman spanned the bow simply by straightening his back. This remained the most popular system until the increasing draw weights to be generated meant that mechanical assistance was necessary. Devices employed included the "goat's foot" lever, a cranequin, and windlasses, particularly for larger crossbows such as those mounted on walls. Such devices had the advantage that they allowed the user to span the bow with just his arms, making it viable for cavalry to use and reload a crossbow without dismounting.

The firing rate of the longbow was far superior to that of the crossbow, to which is attributed the triumph of the English longbowmen over the Genoese crossbowmen at the Battle of Crécy in 1346. Crossbowmen on the battlefield sheltered behind large shields known as *pavises* when reloading, offering them protection when they were most vulnerable but further limiting their mobility. On the other hand, the crossbow could be drawn in advance and held cocked and ready until needed. It also required less room for deployment, and so was better suited for use as a siege weapon than on the battlefield.

The equalizer

Perhaps the greatest advantage of the crossbow was that, athough it required years of training and practice to attain a high level of skill with the longbow, a soldier could become expert in the use of a crossbow in a week. This and the armor-piercing power of the crossbow made it something of an equalizer — with a single shot a lowly commoner could bring down a lord despite all his expensive armor and training. Such a democratizing weapon inspired fear and loathing in the upper classes.

In response to the armor-piercing danger of the crossbow, knights adopted ever heavier and thicker armor, graduating from chain mail to full plate. Yet even the strongest plate mail could not block a bolt from a steel bow. At times crossbows were *too* effective. At the Battle of Lincoln in 1217, for instance, the crossbowmen were ordered to target the enemy horses and not the riders, since knights were much more valuable as captives to be ransomed than as

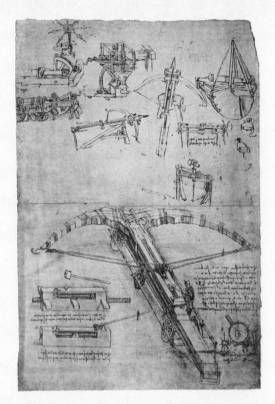

A sketch from one of Leonardo da Vinci's notebooks of a giant crossbow, conceived mainly as a psychological weapon to strike fear into enemy troops.

A short bow or "prod" was attached at right angles to a stock or tiller (usually of wood but sometimes of metal). A nut, sometimes of bone or ivory, held the string when the bow was spanned (drawn), with the projectile, known as a bolt or quarrel, fitting into a groove in the stock. The bow itself could be made of wood or a composite of horn or whalebone, laths of yew and tendon. From the 14th century, steel bows started to appear. The bowstring was made from a rigid, twisted cord, usually of hemp.

The crossbow's great medieval competitor was the longbow (see page 66), and the two had complementary advantages and disadvantages.

corpses. Nonetheless there were high-profile noble casualties, most notably Richard I "the Lionheart" of England, who died from an infected crossbow-bolt wound sustained at the Siege of Châlus-Chabrol in 1199. (Interestingly, the Lionheart may not have been the first English king to be killed by a crossbow bolt — a crossbow may have dispatched William Rufus, said to have died in a hunting accident.) Crossbowmen who fell into the hands of enemy knights were cruelly treated — either mutilated or executed.

Hateful to God

The crossbow was so unpopular with the establishment that in 1139 the Church tried to ban the use of the crossbow by Christians against other Christians. Pope Innocent II denounced the crossbow as "hateful to God and unfit for Christians." The English Magna Carta of 1215 incorporated a promise that "once peace is restored we will banish from the kingdom all foreign-born ... crossbowmen," although the significance of this is undermined by the fact that a year later the royal signatory, King John, hired a company of foreign crossbowmen.

Between 1370 and the introduction of the handgun c. 1470, the steel crossbow was the most powerful weapon of war available to the individual. Although its limitations saw it replaced when firearms became available, the crossbow had played an important role in realigning the balance of power on the battlefield between infantry and cavalry. Better than early guns for hunting because it was silent and more resistant to wet weather, the crossbow remained popular for hunting long after being displaced by the gun from the battlefield. The majority of surviving antique crossbows date to this period and were used for hunting. In China, crossbows survived into the modern era. The Chinese repeating crossbow, or *chukonu*, held bolts in a wooden magazine that sat on top of the stock, and was loaded by pulling back a lever. Accounts suggest it may have been used as long ago as the second century CE and as recently as the Sino-Japanese War of 1894–95.

A man cocking a crossbow using a combination of toe loop or "claw" and a mechanical ratchet.

15

LONGBOW

Type:

Projectile weapon

Social ■

Political

Tactical ■

Technical

c. 13th century

The longbow was a simple but devastating evolution of the millennia-old self bow; it is loosely defined as a bow that is as tall as a man (sometimes taller!), with a deep D-shaped cross section that has a depth to width ratio of 3:1. This deceptively straightforward weapon is credited by some with being responsible for ending the dominance of mounted knights on the battlefields of Europe and restoring the vital role of infantry.

Strong men of Wales

The longbow is said to have developed in the Welsh Marches — the regions along the border between England and Wales — in the 12th century. In fact, there is archaeological evidence of longbow use around Europe from prehistoric times, but Welsh longbowmen would indeed come to form an essential element of English armies up until the 16th century. The longbow was distinguished by its great length: over 6 feet (1.8 m). Longbows recovered from the wreck of the Tudor warship *Mary Rose* ranged from 6 feet, 1 inch (1.87 m) to 6 feet, 10 inches (2.11 m), considerably taller than the average height of a man at the time.

Made primarily from long staves of yew, cut to ensure that the back of the bow was of springy sapwood and the belly of denser heartwood, the longbow was tapered with great care, and strung with hemp whipped with light linen cord. The great length of the bow meant that it had a long draw, which in turn generated enormous pull weights comparable with a crossbow. The *Mary Rose* bows had draws estimated at 150 to 160 pounds (667–712 newtons), giving them a range of as much as 360 yards (329 m), although

generally they were most effective at around 247 yards (226 m). Compare this to the average pull of a modern sporting longbow at around 60 to 70 pounds (267–311 newtons). A longbow could fire an arrow 3 feet (1 m) long with a heavy bodkin head that could pierce chain mail or kill a horse from over 219 yards (200 m) away — it could generate around a third of the power of a modern Colt revolver. William de Braose, an English knight fighting the Welsh, reported in 1188 that an arrow from a longbow had pierced his chain mail and clothes, passed through his thigh and saddle, and penetrated his horse. Crucially, the longbow achieved a superior rate of fire to the crossbow by a factor of 12 to one or more and in the hands of a skilled bowman it offered greater accuracy than the muskets that were in use at the time of the American Revolution.

But this was its major drawback: the strength and skill needed to operate it required many years of training. Seeking to ensure that there would be a ready pool of skilled bowmen, English governments passed numerous ordinances obliging men to train with the

longbow. Since it was considered unchivalrous to kill from a distance, the longbow was considered to be a weapon of the lower classes; hence an English law ordering all men earning less than 100 pence a year to own a longbow. Archery was made compulsory whereas other sports were banned; for instance, soccer was repeatedly banned by kings from Edward II to Edward IV in an attempt to force young men to keep practicing with the bow. Deformities in skeletons of the period testify to the physical toll of long years of training with the bow.

The Hundred Years' War

It was in the century-long conflict between the English and French that the longbow would make its greatest mark, after the English king Edward III recognized its usefulness and developed new tactics to take advantage. The bow's first notable success was at the Battle of Crécy in 1346, where the French outnumbered the English by more than two to one, but the English army included 11,000 archers. The French had 6,000 crack Genoese crossbowmen, but their initial volley landed short of the English bowmen. The chronicler Jean Froissart recalled the English response: "The English archers took a step forward and loosed off a hail of arrows which pierced through arms, heads, and jaws. The Genoese [crossbowmen] were immediately defeated and many cut the cords of their bows while others cast them to the ground and retreated."

The withdrawing Genoese blocked the advance of the French knights; many were struck down by their own side, while the English bowmen continued to fire into the thick of the crowd.

In fact, the warning signs had been there for the French from the very start of the Hundred Years' War. In the first action of the conflict in Flanders near Cadsand in 1337, the Earl of Derby used his longbowmen to drive off the Flemish crossbowmen lining the quays, who were forced to retreat under a hail of missiles while the English army came ashore. Eighty years later longbowmen would record their most famous victory, at Agincourt. Here, in 1415, a French army of over 20,000 men was destroyed by an English army of fewer than

An illustration of Jean de Froissard's account of the Battle of Crécy, showing the English longbowmen overmatching their crossbow-wielding enemies.

8,000, many of them archers. Able to fire up to 12 arrows a minute, the English poured as many as 30,000 arrows into the front ranks of the French force in the first minute alone. Boggy ground and a screen of sharpened stakes hindered French mobility. Of a force of 800 men-at-arms under the Duke of Brabant, detailed to clear away the archers, 660 were cut down before reaching them.

Victory at Crécy, Agincourt, and other battles was not due solely to the tactical advantages of the longbow, but to the overall tactical system perfected by Edward III, in which archers were supported by infantry. Infantry protected the archers and closed with the opposing front once the longbows had done their work, unhorsing knights and compressing the enemy divisions.

The eventual decline of the longbow was partly attributable to the rise of gunpowder. In one of the decisive conflicts at the end of the Hundred Years' War, at Formigny in 1450, English archers were dislodged from their defensive positions by skillful French use of cannons, and then ridden down by cavalry. But the main reason that gunpowder weapons superseded the longbow was that they were easier to use. Unlike the longbow, the arquebus and musket did not require years of intensive strength conditioning and archery training.

The longbow was not exclusively Welsh or English — here, French bowmen demonstrate the latest in medieval millinery.

"The English archers took a step forward and loosed off a hail of arrows which pierced through arms, heads, and jaws."

THE *CHRONICLES* OF JEAN FROISSART, C. 1370

16

Inventor(s):
Western Europeans

EARLY CANNON

Type:

Firearm

Social

Political ■

Tactical

Technical ■

"A marvel except for the bronze bullets, which are shot with spewing flames and awful-sounding thunder … human madness copied the inimitable thunderbolt."

PETRARCH, *ON THE REMEDIES OF GOOD AND BAD FORTUNE* (C. 1360)

c. 1300

Gunpowder, generally known as black powder, had been discovered by the Chinese in the first millennium CE. By around 1100 they were using it on the battlefield, but only in the form of rockets, flame-throwers, and incendiary devices. Firearms, which is to say weapons that use the explosive force of gunpowder to hurl or shoot projectiles, were known to the Chinese, but had greatest impact in Europe. Although it took several generations for them to progress from battlefield curiosity to tactical linchpin, their advent would change warfare and society forever.

Thunderers

Gunpowder disseminated from China to the medieval Islamic world, where the Arabs developed a device called a *madfaa*. This may have been simply a form of flame-thrower akin to a Roman candle, but some sources describe it as the earliest, extremely crude firearm, with the powder sitting in a bowl atop which sat a large stone ball, like an egg on an eggcup. Possibly inspired by this, or possibly working independently, Europeans came up with the *pot-de-fer* (iron jug), a bottle- or vase-shaped iron vessel into the end of which was rammed a metal dart. This at least is the device pictured in a 1326 manuscript presented to Edward III of England, who is said to have used similar weapons in Scotland in 1326. Shortly after this,

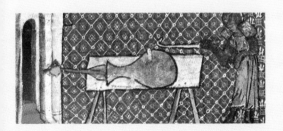

The earliest European depiction of a cannon, from a manuscript by Walter de Milemete in 1326.

one of the first historically confirmed uses of a firearm in warfare occurred, in 1331 at Cividale del Friuli, Italy, where a chronicler recorded: "setting vessels against the city … those from a distance shot with a *sclopus* against the ground and did no damage." A *sclopus* or *sclopetum* was the Latin term for the Italian *schioppo* (thunderer), although this later came to mean a "hand-gonne" rather than a cannon.

The first "true" cannons were bombards, constructed from iron in a similar process to barrel-making. Iron hoops were welded together around iron staves to produce either short-barreled bombards with wide muzzles, or long-barreled ones that were more tubelike. These fired stone shot, with the stones sometimes bound in iron hoops to stop them shattering on firing. They sat on wooden stocks or immobile "carriages"; the earliest ones may simply have been propped up on heaps of earth. Early bombards may have been the guns in use at Cividale, and the chronicler Jean Froissart claimed that the English deployed some at Crécy in 1346. By around

Mons Meg, the great iron bombard of Edinburgh Castle, which saw action just once and blew up in 1681 when fired to celebrate a royal birthday.

1360 they were widespread enough for the Italian writer Petrarch to claim that cannons had become "as common and familiar as other kinds of arms." Hand-gonnes were first mentioned in 1364; at first they consisted of little more than a metal tube lashed to a wooden stock and fired much like their larger cousins.

Iron hoop bombards could achieve monstrous dimensions. The famous Mons Meg gun now in Edinburgh Castle, presented to James II of Scotland in 1457, is 13 feet (4 m) long, weighs 6.7 tons (6 tonnes) and could fire a stone ball weighing 330 pounds (150 kg) nearly 2 miles (over 3 km). A hooped-iron bombard named Basilica, constructed for Ottoman sultan Mohammed II during his assault on Constantinople, had a bore 36 inches (91 cm) across, required 200 men and 60 oxen to move, and fired a ball weighing 1,598 pounds (725 kg) over 1 mile (about 2 km). It took an hour to load and was supposed to fire just seven times a day, but it fell apart after its first few shots.

For whom the bell tolls

It was quickly discovered that the method used to cast bells could also be used to cast-bronze cannons. Where iron-hoop cannons frequently fell apart or blew up, cast-bronze cannons had greater integrity and a greater degree of standardization, although it took 200 years for casters to realize that if they reused the same mold they could achieve some consistency of bore and use the same size balls.

A large cannon might use 3.3 to 4.5 tons (3–4 tonnes) of bronze and the gun carriage itself, with bands, bolts, chain, and hook of iron, weighed almost as much. So even after wheeled cannons were introduced in the Hussite wars of 1419–24, they were far from mobile. Cannons were given names, and their gunners were generally hired hands who owed allegiance not to their employers but to the cannon itself, the source of their livelihood. Sometimes employers would hire foot soldiers to make sure they didn't remove their cannon at the first sign of trouble.

Really useful cannon

A major advance came in the mid-15th century when the Bureau brothers of France introduced cast-iron cannonballs, which fitted more tightly into the cannon bore and so were shot rather than simply tossed. Also, iron balls were stronger and more shatter-resistant than stone ones; smaller balls could be fired with more destructive results, whereas siege trains could become more mobile because they had to contend with less massive ammunition.

The cannon now became a decisive weapon of war, making its mark in the defining battles of the Hundred Years' War. At Formigny in 1450 cannons drove the English longbowmen from their positions, making it possible for the French cavalry to ride them down, whereas at Castillon in 1453 the last English army was destroyed by a French army equipped with artillery. But it was as siege weapons that early cannons made their greatest impact. In his reconquest of Normandy in 1449–50, Charles VII racked up 60 successful siege operations in 16 months thanks to his cannons, whereas at the Fall of Constantinople in 1453, the Ottomans finally overcame the formerly impenetrable walls of Byzantium due to their great ordnance. The siege train of Mohammed II included 56 cannons and 12 great bombards.

Around the end of the 15th century a number of technological advances came together at once. As well as cast-iron shot, the quality of gunpowder began to improve and new cannon casting techniques led to the creation of the first artillery pieces mobile enough to keep up with a campaigning army. These were the "new" cannons of Charles VIII of France, which pioneering military historian Hans Delbrück called the first "really useful cannon." In 1494, Charles VIII launched an invasion of Italy, armed with cannons that had integral trunnions (projecting support pivots), allowing the cannon to sit on a lightweight two-wheeled carriage. This in turn made the cannon both mobile and much quicker to "lay," or aim, because it was much easier to elevate or depress the muzzle than with the previous wooden trough-style carriages. These cannons would decisively demonstrate how the new artillery principle was bringing to an end the age of castles. When Charles' guns were turned on the Neapolitan castle of Monte San Giovanni, which had previously withstood a conventional siege for seven years, it fell within eight hours. Italy was defeated inside three months.

On the battlefield, however, the effect of early cannons were still limited when the terrain allowed infantry to stay mobile. On two occasions where this was not the case, Ravenna in 1512 and Marignano in 1515, French armies scored great victories because their cannons were able to lay waste to Spanish and Swiss enemy formations that were unable to maneuver properly because of entrenchments and earthworks. But even with their two-wheeled carriages, cannons were still too unwieldy to be redeployed on the battlefield: once a battery was set in position, it would have to remain there for the duration of the battle. This meant that the tactical role of artillery on the battlefield would remain restricted until the 18th century.

17

Inventor(s):

Prehistoric man

RENAISSANCE PIKE

Type:

Pole-arm

Social ■

Political

Tactical ■

Technical

15th century

A pike is essentially a very long spear. Its history powerfully illustrates how the simplest weapon can achieve devastating results with the right tactics. Indeed, its simplicity may help to account for the remarkable tactical versatility that saw the pike play a key role in battles from the 13th century right up to the late 17th century.

Poor man's weapon

As long spears, pikes effectively date back to the earliest prehistoric times, but if a "true" pike is one with a metal spear point and a very elongated shaft (pikes could be up to 20 feet/6 m long in the 16th century), the earliest example to make its mark on history must be the *sarissa* of the Macedonian phalanx, used to such devastating effect by Alexander the Great. In fact, the Macedonian model, with an aggressive, fast-moving phalanx backed up by cavalry support, was to prove the inspiration for pikemen of the Renaissance.

On the medieval battlefield, the pike was viewed as the quintessential poor man's weapon. Where the landed noble could afford a horse, armor and a sword, forces such as the Flemish militia or the peasant armies of lowland Scotland could not. Their solution to counteract the strengths of the mounted knight was the age-old tactic of a long, sharp stick. Armed with pikes they could keep the cavalry at a distance, compensating for their lack of armor and preventing the knight from bringing his horse and superior weaponry to bear.

The most notable successes of the medieval period for pike-wielding armies were the battles of Stirling Bridge (1297) and Bannockburn (1314) in the Wars of Scottish Independence, and the Battle of Courtrai, or Golden Spurs (1302). In all these cases armies of mainly lowborn soldiers defeated aristocratic armies. At Stirling Bridge the Scots under William Wallace took full advantage of a tactical blunder by the English commander, John de Warenne, who sent his army across the bridge into the teeth of Scottish opposition. Wallace's pikemen charged the English when they were halfway across, and with no room to maneuver the English knights were run down. This was the first battle in Europe where an army of pike-wielding commoners defeated a feudal host. Just five years later the feat would be repeated, where doughty Flemish townspeople armed with *geldon* pikes rebuffed charging French knights before inflicting a heavy defeat on them.

In the manner of the Almayns

These medieval victories for the pike-wielding infantryman are credited as key steps in the redress of the balance between cavalry and infantry in the Middle Ages. Feudal armies responded to the challenge of the pike-block, as the preferred formation of pikemen came to be known, by exploiting its weakness: unable to afford armor or carry shields, pikemen were highly vulnerable to ranged weapons. At Falkirk in 1298, for instance, Wallace's schiltrons ("great circles" — the Scottish version of the pike block) were cut down by English archers and he was defeated.

To overcome the threat of ranged weapons, pike-blocks needed to become more aggressive and more mobile, and this was the innovation introduced by the Swiss, who transformed the pike into the most feared weapon in Europe. In *The Art of War*, Machiavelli advanced an explanation for the Swiss development of pike-block tactics. Forced to fight for their freedom against the heavy cavalry of the imperial Austrian armies, the Swiss, with scant resources and a relatively egalitarian set of troops, devised tactics to best suit themselves. They looked to the ancient model of Alexander's Macedonian phalanx, armed themselves with the cheap and readily available pike, and trained themselves to move at speed without losing coordination. The result was an offensive tactic of shocking success that dominated the battlefield of its era and terrified opposing troops. Their tactics were so impressive that the Scots under James IV sought to ape what they called "fighting in the manner of the Almayns" (Germans, by which was meant the Swiss) in their war with the English. Unfortunately, the Scottish made some fatal errors in their attempt to mimic the Swiss tactics, such as failing to employ flanking artillery, bowmen, and advanced skirmishers, essential to break up enemy formations, allowing the pike-block charge to do its work. The disaster at Flodden in 1513 graphically illustrated how successful use of the pike depended on very precise execution of a complete tactical system.

With their new pike tactics, the Swiss shocked Europe by destroying the Burgundians in a series of battles in 1476–77. Swiss success inspired imitators, and around this time the pike was adopted by the German Landsknechts, a mercenary force noted for their flamboyant dress sense. The Landsknecht used a pike with an ash shaft around 18 feet (5.5 m) long, fitted with a 10-inch (25 cm) steel tip and often decorated with the tail of a fox or other animal for good luck. In the wars of the period, battles often saw the Landsknechts pitted against the Swiss, and an arms race in pike lengths saw dimensions balloon to 20 feet (6 m) long. The shaft would be made of cured ash and tapered toward the tip in an attempt to reduce the terminal weight, but sagging was inevitably an issue.

"the issue of a battle might be decided by archers or pikemen"

M. Vale, War and Chivalry (1981)

Pike and shot

By now a crucial element had been added to the pike-army mix: firearms. Pikes found a new battlefield role in concert with arquebuses and later muskets. Pikemen protected musketeers, who were vulnerable, especially to cavalry charges and particularly while reloading; the musketeers then cleared the way for the pikemen to advance.

The Landsknechts began to gain the upper hand on the Swiss by virtue of their willingness to improve the ratio of arquebusiers to pikemen, but they in turn would be superseded by the Spanish development of *tercio* tactics. From 1505 the Spanish had fielded *colunelas*, thousand-strong mixed units of pikemen,

A late 17th-century manual of martial arts shows the correct stance for a pikeman.

arquebusiers, and sword and shield infantry; by the 1530s these units had swollen to *tercios* of 3,000 men or more, still with a central block of pikemen, with arquebusiers around the outside and clumps of them at the corners. A *tercio* was a formidable, self-supporting fighting force, able to roll across the battlefield like a mobile fortress, equipped to cope with all styles of opponent attacking from any direction.

Tercio tactics carried the day at the Battle of Pavia in 1525, where the French king Francis I — obsessed with chivalry and known as the "knightly king" — badly misunderstood the new tactical realities of firearm-centered warfare. Just when it seemed that his cannons were about to win the day for him, he led his cavalry in front of his own guns, forcing them to cease firing, and then fell prey to the lethal combination of pike and musket. Surrounded by Hapsburg pike and shot, the French knights were hemmed in by a bristling wall of spear tips and shot down by arquebus volleys. Francis himself was taken prisoner and Pavia proved to be one of the worst defeats in military history.

The pike declined slowly in the 17th century as muskets improved and became more ubiquitous. Gradually, the ratio of firearms to pole-arms shifted, but the pike continued to be an important battlefield weapon long after almost every other bladed weapon had become obsolete. It was abandoned by the Germans and British only in 1697, when they officially adopted the zigzag bayonet for their muskets.

18

MATCHLOCK

Type:

Firearm

Social ■

Political

Tactical

Technical ■

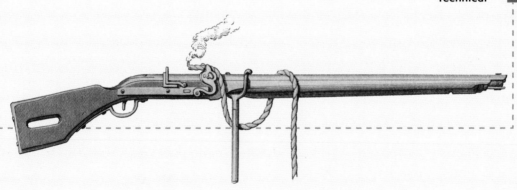

"… an instrument new, as you know, and necessary."

MACHIAVELLI, *THE ART OF WAR*, BOOK 2 (1521)

Mid to late 15th century

The matchlock derived its name from the two elements, "match" and "lock," where the latter was the general term for the mechanism that set off the charge in a firearm (probably deriving from its resemblance to a door lock mechanism) and the former was a slow-burning piece of cord. The matchlock was the first effective handheld firearm. It was clumsy, dirty, difficult, and dangerous, but it transformed the nature of war at tactical and strategic levels.

Serpentines and saltpeter

The first portable firearms, or "hand-gonnes," were essentially miniature cannons: muzzle-loaded iron tubes affixed to wooden stocks, fired by applying a smoldering "slow match" (a length of cord soaked in alcohol and coated in saltpeter, potassium nitrate, to achieve a slow but steady burn) to a touch hole, a tiny hole through to the internal charge. It generally required one man to hold the cannon (and suffer the recoil), and another to light the touch hole. The resulting shot was likely to be wildly inaccurate.

In the mid to late 15th century, possibly as early as 1411 and probably in Spain, the hand-gonne was transformed into an effective firearm by a simple but effective device: the serpentine matchlock. A pivoted S-shaped lever, the serpentine holds the burning match at one end, equivalent to the hammer of a modern gun, whereas the bottom half acts as the trigger. Pulling the trigger causes the serpentine to dip the smoldering match into a priming pan — a small pan filled with powder — causing a flash in the pan, which is transmitted via the touch hole to the charge inside the gun. The operator is thus freed from having to look for the touchhole, allowing him to sight on the target.

The first gun to be fitted with a matchlock was the arquebus or hackbut, a name that probably derived from the German *Hakenbuchse*, "hook-gun" (possibly named for a hook that allowed the gun to be braced on the edge of a wall to help absorb recoil). The Spanish fired the arquebus from the shoulder, but to start with other nations fired it from the chest. It had many disadvantages. Loading and firing an arquebus was laborious, requiring up to 96 separate motions. Even in 1600 it still took 10 to 15 minutes to load an arquebus. When the match was lowered the proverbial "flash in the pan" often failed to ignite the main charge, but there was also a risk that the match might set off the priming powder too soon, causing accidents. The gun needed cleaning between shots. It could not be used in wet weather, and the glowing match gave away the location of the arquebusier at night or in ambush. The smoothbore barrel of the gun restricted its accurate range, typically to less than 900 feet (274 m). As late as 1550 an expert longbow archer could shoot faster and more accurately than any gunner.

Set against this was the simple fact that a matchlock placed an unanswerable killing tool in the hands of any common soldier who could learn actions by rote. All the chivalry and skill of the most highly trained knight in Europe was of no avail against a musket ball, which could pierce even the strongest plate armor.

Other names for shoulder-fired matchlocks included *caliver* and *culverin*. Muskets were heavier versions of the arquebus, requiring a forked rest to hold up the muzzle while firing. At the start of the matchlock era, in the early

stages of the Italian Wars, about one-sixth of the Spanish army was equipped with firearms — either arquebus or musket. In drawing up plans for raising a Florentine army in 1506, Machiavelli specified that for every 100 infantry there should be at least 10 *scoppietteri* (light matchlock gunners). The explosion in the popularity of the matchlock is graphically attested by comparing the weapons found on two Tudor shipwrecks separated by less than 50 years. The wreck of the *Mary Rose*, which sank in 1545, proved to contain over a hundred longbows but very few firearms. The *Alderney* was a ship that sank in 1592; on its wreck the majority of the weapons were firearms. The proportion of firearms with which an army was equipped would increase as the technology of the firearm slowly improved, and solutions were found to the problems posed by the match itself, in the form of the first flintlocks.

The new art of war

For all its difficulties the matchlock engendered profound changes in the nature of warfare. Even more so than the crossbow (see page 62), the new firearms were profoundly democratizing weapons. Relatively cheap to manufacture, matchlocks could be widely distributed among the infantry. Anybody could now blast a hole through the armor of the most noble knight, prompting similar reactions to those experienced earlier by crossbow archers (see page 65). For instance, when lowborn gunners killed some of his mounted nobles, late-15th-century Italian commander Gian Paolo Vitelli decreed that all captured arquebusiers should

Illustrations from a 17th-century manual for trainee musketeers.

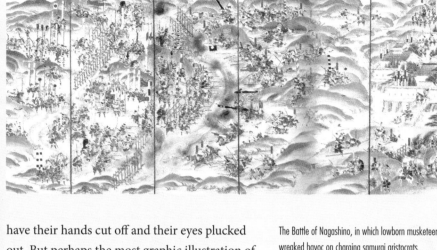

have their hands cut off and their eyes plucked out. But perhaps the most graphic illustration of how the matchlock changed the class dynamic on the battlefield came from the other side of the world, at the 1575 Battle of Nagashino in Japan. Here 1,500 to 3,000 arquebusiers, under Odo Nobunaga, destroyed the charging samurai of Takeda Katsuyori, upending the traditional social order of Japanese warfare.

The inevitable popularity of the matchlock in turn had important strategic consequences because of the material and logistical demands engendered by the new firearms. A musket, with its ramrod, rest, and ammunition, was heavier than, for instance, the weapons of a Roman legionary. So although a legionary had been able to carry his gear and around two weeks of rations (totaling around 80 pounds/36 kg), an arquebusier, whose armor alone weighed almost as much as the Roman's entire kit, could not carry his own food. He also needed a central authority to supply gunpowder, shot, and parts and maintenance for his weapon. Armies now depended on baggage trains as never before, and

The Battle of Nagashino, in which lowborn musketeers wreaked havoc on charging samurai aristocrats.

were hence slower and less self-sufficient; supply lines became vital. The Hapsburgs, fighting from a base in Spain but with supply lines extending to the Netherlands and Italy, soon made this unhappy discovery. The art of war was steadily becoming the science of logistics.

Operating an arquebus could be an elaborate performance. Along with his gun and sword, an arquebusier carried a flask of gunpowder and a supply of match cord, a ramrod, scrapers, a bullet extractor and rags for loading and cleaning, bullet lead and a brass mold for casting musket balls, and a flint and steel for lighting matches. Many arquebusiers would be accompanied by an attendant who carried some of the load and kept a fire going.

19

SMALLPOX (AND GERM WARFARE)

Type:

Biological warfare

Social ■
Political ■
Tactical
Technical

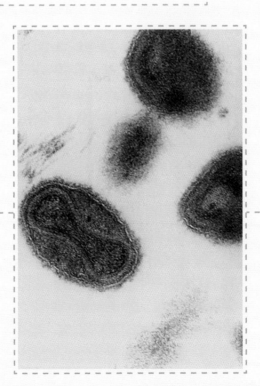

16th century

Smallpox was a viral disease that has now been eradicated thanks to a global public health initiative. As the cause of one of the most devastating epidemics in history, it can claim to have been the primary weapon of European colonial powers in their conquest of the Americas. On at least one occasion it was spread intentionally as a deliberate form of biological warfare.

Mountains of dead

Smallpox was not the first germ to be used as a weapon. In the Middle Ages, besiegers would sometimes use trebuchets and other siege engines to hurl the corpses of horses and even humans into besieged cities or forts, in an attempt to spread corruption and foul humors (there being little active appreciation of the biology of contagion at the time). The most notorious such episode was at the Siege of Caffa, in 1346, where the Tartars (the generic name employed by the Europeans to describe Mongols; in this case the Golden Horde) besieged a city in the Crimea but were afflicted by a terrible plague: the Black Death. According to the account — probably secondhand — of the Genoese Gabriele de' Mussi, what seemed at first to the Christian defenders like divine providence striking down the heathens soon turned into a nightmarish episode of biological terror. After three years of the siege, "the trapped Christians … hemmed in by an immense army … could hardly draw breath." De' Mussi also claimed that Genoese merchants fleeing the city carried the plague to the Mediterranean, from where it spread across Europe with devastating results (over a third of the population would die in the pandemic). In other words, biological attack by the Tartars was the direct cause of the Black Death. However, University of California historian Mark Wheeler argues that, although "the claim that biological warfare was used at Caffa is plausible and provides the best explanation of the entry of plague into the city … the entry of plague into Europe from the Crimea likely occurred independent of this event."

Crowd-sourced

Even more deadly than the Black Death was the pandemic that swept the Americas in the decades after the first contact with Europeans in the Age of Exploration. Smallpox was a highly contagious viral disease, which caused spots that developed into pustules, which left deeply pitted scars known as pocks. In the disease's most severe form the pustules would join together in a great blister covering the body, or there would be extensive bleeding all over the body; these were known as confluent and

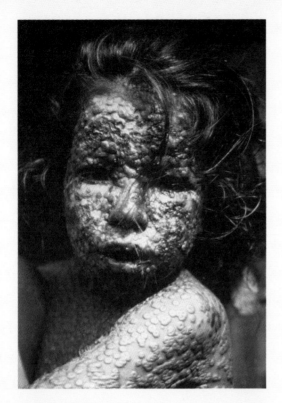

The gruesome and disfiguring effects of smallpox are clearly shown in this photo of a pox sufferer from Bangladesh.

hemorrhagic smallpox, respectively. Normal smallpox had a death rate of around 30 percent, whereas the confluent and hemorrhagic forms were almost always fatal.

Smallpox is believed to have evolved in South Central Asia around the first century CE, and to have been a "crowd disease": one that evolved as the result of close proximity between humans and livestock, together with the buildup of large, concentrated populations, which allowed the virus to jump from one type of herd (e.g., cattle or horses) to another (village- and city-dwelling humans). Although it caused severe morbidity and mortality in Old World populations for centuries, and may have been the organism behind various mystery plagues of antiquity, populations in Eurasia and Africa built up a degree of resistance to it through constant exposure and selection pressure.

The population of the Americas, with a comparatively short history of human settlement and no tradition of large-scale animal husbandry, had never encountered the disease and had no immunity. When Europeans brought the disease to the New World the effects were devastating and changed the course of history. For instance, when the Spanish conquistadors under Hernán Cortez besieged the Aztec capital Tenochtitlán in 1521, the Amerindians were also contending with a smallpox epidemic. Some 50,000 Aztecs were said to have perished from disease by the time the Spaniards entered the devastated city. The pandemic may have destroyed up to 90 percent of the indigenous population of Central and South America. North America suffered similar ravages.

The desired effect

The New World smallpox pandemic may have involved inadvertent "weaponization" of the disease, but there is hard evidence that colonial forces also engaged in deliberate germ warfare. In the French and Indian War of 1756–63, the commander of British forces in North America was Lord Jeffrey Amherst. Surviving letters show him discussing with Colonel Henry Bouquet a strategy for wiping out the Native Americans. In a letter of July 16th, 1763, Amherst wrote:

> P.S. You will Do well to try to Innoculate the Indians by means of Blanketts, as well as to try Every other method that can serve to Extirpate this Execrable Race. I should be very glad your Scheme for Hunting them Down by Dogs could take Effect, but England is at too great a Distance to think of that at present.

A couple of months earlier, on May 24th, the journal of William Trent, commander of the Pittsburgh local militia, records that: " ... we gave them two Blankets and an Handkerchief out of the Small Pox Hospital. I hope it will have the desired effect." Within months the local Indian population had indeed been ravaged by smallpox.

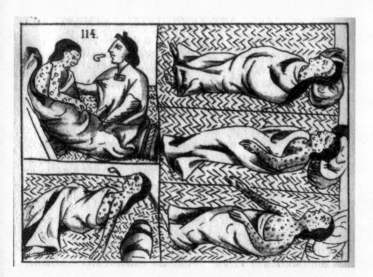

An Aztec depiction of the hideous plague that afflicted them in the wake of the Spanish conquest.

20

Inventor(s):

The knife makers of Bayonne

BAYONET

Type:

Blade weapon

Social

Political

Tactical ■

Technical

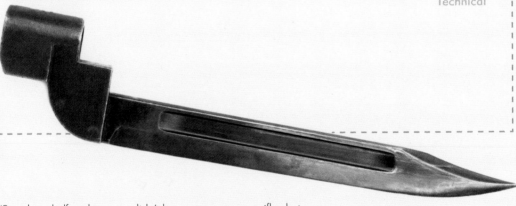

"For about half an hour you didn't hear a cannon or a rifle shot …
[only] some inexpressible roar of thousands of brave soldiers in hand
to hand struggle, mixing and cutting each other up."

RUSSIAN OFFICER DENIS DAVIDOV, BATTLE OF EYLAU, 1807

Late 16th century

A bayonet is a blade that can fit onto the end of a musket or rifle, enabling the infantryman to use the same weapon for firing and close-quarter combat. The name supposedly derives from the French town of Bayonne, famous for its knife-making, where in the 16th century a hunter's dagger known as *le bayonette de Bayonne* was manufactured. It was distinguished by its tapering hilt and wide cross-guard, which allowed the hunter, as a last resort if faced by an angry boar and no time to reload, to jam the hilt into the muzzle of his gun and use it as a boar spear.

Plug ugly

Whether or not this tale is true, the bayonet solved some of the problems associated with the adoption of the musket. Muskets took a considerable time to reload, during which the infantryman was vulnerable, and if cavalry or other troops closed in on him, he could not fire fast enough to defend himself. This was the rationale for the enduring role of the pikeman in 17th-century armies, but the bayonet offered a way to combine the roles of gunner and pikeman in one.

The first record of the use of bayonets comes from around 1647, when French soldiers in the Netherlands were equipped with 12-inch (30 cm) bladed bayonets. The first British troops armed with them were Prince Rupert's Dragoons in 1672. But the plug bayonet had the obvious disadvantage that, once fitted, it prevented the musket from being fired. Soldiers had to choose one or the other, and indecision could be fatal. At the battle of Killiecrankie in 1689, a British force of 4,000 men under General Hugh Mackay was ambushed by a force of Highlanders who charged downhill at them. "The Highlanders are of such quick motion that if a Battalion keep up

his fire till they be near to make sure of [hitting] them, they are upon it before our men can come to the second defense, which is the bayonet in the muzzle of the musket." (From *Soldiers: A History of Men in Battle*, by John Keegan and Richard Holmes.) Half the British soldiers were lost in the ensuing debacle.

By this time at least one solution had already been invented: the ring bayonet, where the barrel of the gun fitted through rings attached to the hilt of the bayonet. A much better locking mechanism was the socket bayonet, invented c. 1687, where a spearheadlike triangular blade was attached to an arm projecting from the side of a sleeve or socket that fit over the barrel of the gun. A zigzag slot cut into the socket engaged with studs on the barrel of the gun, which could double as a fore-sight. The basic pattern of the bayonet was now established.

Were bayonets pointless?

Adding a long steel blade to the end of a musket ruined the balance of the weapon and further

BAYONET

Bayonet charge during the American Civil War.

degraded the accuracy of fire (see page 79). The received wisdom amongst military historians seems to be that the bayonet was largely symbolic, and that it was of little practical value, with actual bayonet combat being relatively rare. Bayonets were more important for morale than killing power, a point illustrated by George Washington's response on being warned that his planned attack on Trenton would have to be called off because the soldiers' muskets were wet and would not fire: "Tell General Sullivan to use the bayonet. I am resolved to take Trenton." Trenton duly fell, marking a turning point in the War of Independence.

On this basis, size was in fact important; the short spike bayonet issued with some Second World War British rifles, though quite long

enough for killing, did not inspire confidence and was referred to in derogatory terms as the "pigsticker." On the other hand, larger "sword" bayonets were impractically unwieldy. The bayonet issued with many British rifles in the Second World War was a long and impractical sword bayonet known as the "Indian Pattern"; historian Pierre Berton records that Canadian troops deemed the Indian Pattern good for little more than toasting bread over a campfire.

Blood and guts

Although statistically speaking the bayonet may have played little role in generating casualties, the psychological impact of bayonet combat in an era of distance killing is evident from accounts of conflicts from the American

Revolution to the Second World War and beyond. Describing the gory climax of the Battle of Bunker Hill in 1775, a British officer recorded: "We tumbled over the dead to get at the living, soldiers stabbing some and dashing out the brains of others." One of the most visceral accounts comes from the Battle of Eylau, in 1807, where Russian officer Denis Davidov gave an eyewitness account of what happened when French and Russian corps collided in close-quarters combat:

> Over 20,000 men from both sides were plunging a three-faceted blade into each other … I was a personal witness of this Homeric slaughter … Mounds of dead bodies were piled over with new mounds… this segment of the battle resembled a high parapet …

The machine guns and trench warfare of the First World War rendered the bayonet largely impotent; it was now almost impossible for troops to get close enough to the enemy to need one. The Second World War saw troops regain some mobility, but by this time small-arms had advanced to the point where the bayonet was mostly superfluous. Yet the weapon retained its edge of close-quarter savagery. Historian Antony Beevor relates an incident from the Battle of Stalingrad, where the fighting around Mamayev Kurgan reached particular heights of ferocity: two bodies were dug up — a German and a Soviet soldier, caught in the act of simultaneously stabbing each other with bayonets when they were buried by an exploding shell.

Some modern forces have abandoned the bayonet altogether: the US Army discontinued bayonet training in 2010, although the Marines still insist that the OKC-3S Bayonet "is the weapon of choice when shots can't be fired." British soldiers made bayonet charges in the Falklands, the Gulf War, and in Iraq as recently as 2004, but on the whole the knife bayonet now issued is mainly used for nonbayonet functions, such as wire cutting.

An English sergeant-major demonstrates to American trainees how not to defend against a bayonet thrust.

21

FLINTLOCK

Type:

Firearm

Social

Political ■

Tactical

Technical ■

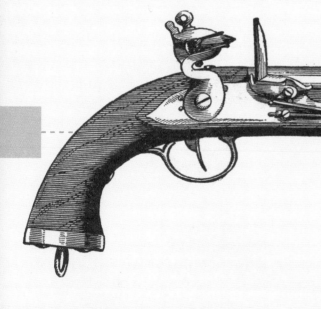

c. 1620

The matchlock had changed the nature of war, but it was far from satisfactory. Gunners had to trail a long cord of burning match from their weapons, which could not be preloaded and held in readiness and were rendered useless by damp weather. For the firearm to become truly ubiquitous as the weapon of the infantryman, new firing mechanisms were needed.

Wheel-lock guns

Around 1515 the wheel lock was invented, possibly in Nuremberg, Germany. The match was replaced with a spring-loaded serrated metal wheel that could be wound like a clock. When released it struck against a "dog" or "cock" — a piece of iron pyrites — striking sparks that would ignite the powder in the pan. Being essentially a precision-engineered clockwork device, the wheel lock was expensive and hard to maintain, and so failed to catch on universally; the American colonists, for instance, preferred matchlocks until the true flintlock arrived. The wheel lock did lead, however, to the first practical pistols (the name possibly derives from the Italian town of Pistoia, where guns were manufactured), also known as "dags," which could be used by men on horseback. Pistols were also adopted by assassins — in 1584, William the Silent of Holland became the first world leader assassinated by a pistol when he was gunned down with a wheel-lock model.

As muskets became lighter they started to replace arquebuses. In the 1560s the Duke of Alva had 15 musketeers to every 100 arquebusiers, but by the Thirty Years' War (1618–48), the army of the Swedish king Gustavus Adolphus was mainly equipped with muskets.

Dogs and cocks

By this time a typical musket had a 4-foot (1.2 m) smoothbore barrel, with a 0.5 to 1 inch (13–25 mm) caliber and an effective range of around 55 yards (50 m). Technology continued to advance. The snaphaunce lock, also known as the "snapping matchlock," had a two-part mechanism consisting of a spring-powered cock and a trigger, giving almost instantaneous firing on pulling the trigger. The name "snaphaunce" came from the Dutch *snap-haan* (pecking fowl or snapping cock). Its development in the late 16th century, alongside similar mechanisms such as the frizzen, miquelet lock, Scandinavian snaplock, and dog lock, paved the way for the introduction of the true flintlock early in the 17th century. In a flintlock the firing mechanism strikes the flint against a steel arm known as the frizzen, and this generates the firing spark. Simultaneously, the falling cock uncovers the priming pan. Flint first substituted for pyrites as early as 1615 in a French musket, and true flintlocks appeared c. 1620.

Although the earliest versions were more expensive and less reliable than the matchlock, the flintlock soon supplanted the matchlock. It was formally adopted by the English in 1682, and soon afterward they developed the Land Pattern Musket, which remained the standard British infantry weapon for 160 years. It was known as the Brown Bess, its name derived from its walnut stock and artificially acid-rusted barrel.

Hold fire

An experiment carried out by the Prussian military in the late 18th century drove home the primary drawback of the smoothbore flintlock. A battalion of infantry fired at a target 100 feet (30 m) long and 6 feet (1.8 m) high, intended to simulate the profile of an advancing enemy battalion. At 225 yards (205 m) just 25 percent of the shots hit their target, rising to 40 percent at 150 yards (137 m) and 60 percent at 75 yards (69 m). In real battlefield conditions the accuracy would likely have been far lower. Hence the famous instruction supposedly given by the American commander at the Battle of Bunker Hill in 1775, "Don't fire 'til you see the whites of their eyes." (In fact, this line was probably invented later.) At Blenheim in 1705 the French did not fire until the leading British officer struck the barricades with his sword just 30 feet (9 m) from their guns.

Commanders cared less about accuracy than volume of fire, hence the importance of relentless drill in training musketeers to load and fire properly. Nonetheless, a gun like the Brown Bess took 40 seconds to load and shoot even in the hands of a proficient gunner. As a result a solider was unlikely to fire more than five rounds before meeting the enemy in hand-to-hand combat, and amid the terror of the battlefield firing rarely went smoothly. Marshal Gouvion Saint-Cyr estimated that a quarter of all French infantry casualties during the Napoleonic Wars were caused by "friendly fire" from men in the rear. Hundreds of muskets recovered from the battlefield at Gettysburg in 1863 had been stuffed with more than one charge of powder and shot, testimony to the panic attendant on combat.

Rifling

Flintlock guns were muzzle-loaded, but this ill-suited the rifling (the incision of helical grooves in the bore of a gun), which imparted spin to a bullet and greatly increased its accuracy. Flintlock rifles were produced but they tended to be more expensive and much harder to load (the bullet needed to be perfectly flush with the bore and so had to be ram-loaded), and were mainly restricted to hunting. One famous exception was the Kentucky rifle, beloved of volunteer marksmen in the Revolutionary Wars, who achieved great feats of marksmanship; for instance, a British officer reported a rifleman had hit his bugler's horse at a range of 400 yards (366 m).

The Flintlock

[A] Frizzen
[B] Cock
[C] Pan
[D] Flint
[E] Clamp for holding flint
[F] Tumbler screw

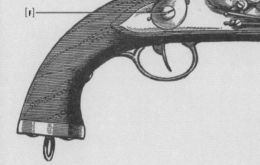

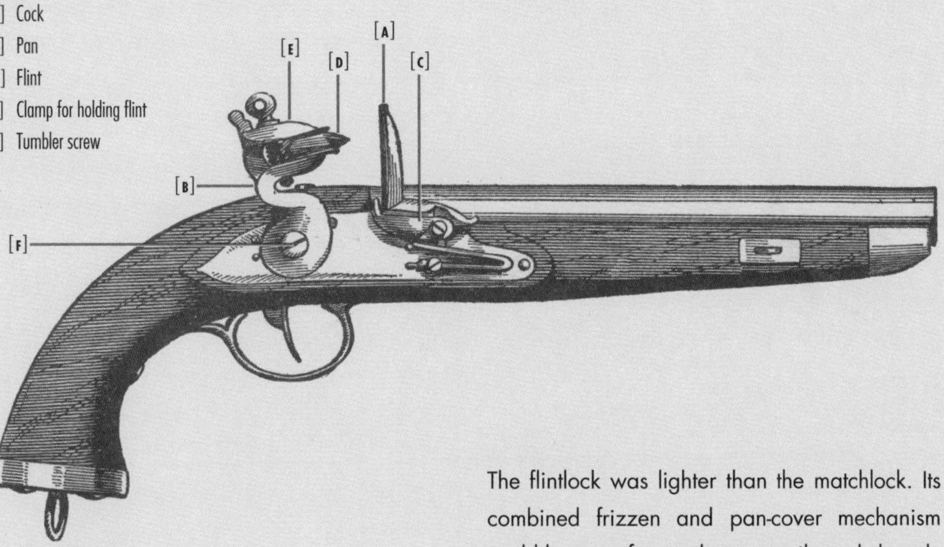

KEY FEATURE:
FLINTLOCK MECHANISM

The flint is held in place by a vice or clamp, which can be opened and tightened by means of a screw. When the gun is cocked, the cock holding the flint is drawn back. When the trigger is pulled, the cock falls, scraping the flint along the face of the frizzen, generating a shower of sparks that falls into the pan below, where it sets off the priming powder.

The flintlock was lighter than the matchlock. Its combined frizzen and pan-cover mechanism could be manufactured more easily and cheaply than the wheel lock, and the covered pan meant the gun could be used in wet weather. Flintlocks also offered a "half-cock" mode, in which the gun could be loaded and primed but not fired, so that it could be preloaded and held in readiness for rapid deployment. These advantages overcame the continuing problems of muzzle-loaded firearms. The flintlock was wildly popular and remarkably durable, persisting as the primary infantry weapon in the Western world from around 1650 to the mid-19th century, and far longer in other parts of the world.

FLINTLOCK

22

Inventor(s):
**Swiss engineer
Jean Maritz**

FIELD
ARTILLERY

Type:

Artillery

Social

Political

Tactical ■

Technical

1755

In the 17th century cannons were still relatively crude. Cannonballs did not fit closely into bores, and so required very large charges to propel them; this in turn meant that barrels had to be thick and heavy. Consequently they remained better suited to siege operations, and in this field of military affairs little changed between 1512 and 1812. But by this time there was an alternative, and it was one that profoundly affected the nature of war — and the attendant butcher's bill.

Lightweights

Field artillery is artillery light and mobile enough to be deployed effectively on the battlefield. In Pavia in 1525, the artillery had been too heavy to play a decisive role in the battle (see page 77), but in the early 17th century this began to change.

In the Thirty Years' War of 1618–48, the preeminent commander was the Swedish king Gustavus Adolphus. He pioneered the use of field artillery, preferring more but lighter cannons. Where Elizabethan armies had used 30-pounders weighing more than 2.2 tons (2 tonnes), Gustavus used guns as small as 3-pounders, known as "leather guns," which weighed just 121 pounds (55 kg), with carriages that could be pulled by two horses rather than the 14 needed for heavy cannon. Where most previous armies were equipped with one heavy cannon for every thousand men, Gustavus had six 9-pounder demi-culverins and two 4-pounders for every thousand. Loaded with canister, these light cannon were intended for use against infantry, not fortifications.

The technical limitations of the guns meant he struggled to get his field artillery in range of the enemy. Nonetheless, the trend for using lighter guns in greater numbers had been established. In the early 18th century, for instance, the Russians reduced the weight of a 12-pounder from 4,045 to 1,082 pounds (1,835 kg to 491 kg), and by 1713 the Russian army had 13,000 artillery pieces. Other commanders attempted to follow Gustavus' lead. In the War of the Spanish Succession, Marlborough sought to detach guns from his "artillery park" and have them accompany the infantry. At Blenheim in 1704, the French guns outmetaled the allies but Marlborough's lighter guns — he had attached two 3-pounders to every English and Dutch battalion — carried the day. Outmaneuvering the heavy French guns, the allied artillery destroyed nine enemy battalions. Even greater success was achieved by Frederick the Great of Prussia during the Seven Years' War (1756–63) — he is considered by many to be the true father of field artillery. Frederick beefed up the role of battalion artillery by instituting dedicated horse artillery units, creating a mobile reserve that could bring artillery to bear rapidly anywhere on the battlefield.

John Churchill, 1st Duke of Marlborough, considered by some historians to have been Britain's greatest general.

Piling up the carcasses

In 1755 came the technical breakthrough that would finally produce field artillery that was light and mobile without sacrificing firepower. Swiss engineer Jean Maritz developed a new barrel-boring technique that produced a tighter fit between the cannon bore and the cannonball. This in turn meant that less powder was needed to produce the same propulsive power, which in turn meant the cannon could have weaker, thinner walls. Seizing on the opportunity afforded by this new technology when he became Inspector of Artillery in 1776, French officer Jean Gribeauval devised a standardized, much lightened system of cannon, limbers, and gun carriages. Where previously a dozen horses had been needed, a typical gun carriage team now used six horses — this would remain stable until horses were replaced by motor tractors in the Second World War.

Gribeauval's reforms would bear fruit in the Napoleonic era, when Napoleon proved himself the first master of field artillery. At Valmy, the first battle in the Revolutionary War in 1792, the artillery duel had inconclusive results. Napoleon later observed that "artillery, like the other arms must be collected in mass if one wishes to obtain a decisive result." His method was to gather his artillery in a *grande batterie* of up to a hundred guns and successively move them as close as possible to the enemy formations. These huge formations could produce devastating effects. At the Battle of Borodino in 1812, Russian artillery officer Radozhitzky recorded his reaction to the French barrage and the Russian counter: "The rounds were so frequent that there were no intervals between them: they soon turned into one continuous roar like a

"The Grenadiers have their muskets, and their hearts and their right-hands. With amazing intrepidity, they … rush into the throat of this Fire-volcano … but it is into the throat of [the Austrians'] iron engines and his tearing billows of cannon-shot that most of them go. Shorn down by the company, by the regiment, in those terrible 800 yards [730 m] …"
THOMAS CARLYLE ON THE BATTLE OF TORGAU, *HISTORY OF FRIEDRICH II OF PRUSSIA* (1760)

Panoramic depiction of the Battle of Waterloo by William Sadler.

thunderstorm, and caused an artificial earthquake." By the end of the battle some 120,000 cannonballs had been fired; Eugène Labaume described how the little spaces between the mounds of dead and wounded "were covered with debris of arms, lances, helmets or cuirasses, or by cannonballs as numerous as hailstones after a violent storm."

Napoleon's command of field artillery is exemplified by his conduct at the Battle of Friedland in 1807. Bottling up Russian infantry in a bend of the River Alle, the French artillery commander General Sénarmont shifted his guns from 600 to 350 to 150 paces, and then just 60 paces from the Russians. Salvoes of canister shot wreaked terrible havoc; the Russians suffered over 50 percent casualties, losing 25,000 men out of 46,000, whereas the French lost just 8,000 out of 80,000. But the ultimate proof of the decisive tactical effects of horse artillery would come at Waterloo. Here, Napoleon outmetaled his opponents with more and bigger guns, but the British horse artillery under Mercer and Bull swung the day with

timely interventions that blasted French cavalry at close range. Mercer described how his cannons "piled up such heaps of carcasses" that the Horse Grenadiers were destroyed, and Wellington admiringly commented, "That is how I like to see horse artillery move." The Napoleonic Wars saw the last major use of traditional bronze and iron field artillery. Steel cannons would arrive in the 1850s, finally making possible the breech-loading cannon, a major step forward in artillery (see page 106).

23

HOWITZER

Type:

Artillery

Social

Political

Tactical ■

Technical ■

18th–20th centuries

A howitzer lies somewhere between a cannon and a mortar. A cannon is used for direct fire, into walls or enemy ranks, and depends on a clear firing trajectory and a line of sight; it has a long range but uses relatively small-caliber shells. A mortar lobs heavy-caliber shells a short distance up and over obstacles — it needs to be quite close to its target. A howitzer has a decent range but fires quite heavy shells; it can be fired over obstacles but from a position some distance behind the front line. It is light and short enough to remain relatively mobile for its caliber, meaning it can be used both for siege artillery and for tactical fire support for infantry.

Hussite howitzers

The name "howitzer" derives from the original incarnation of the gun as a medium-caliber cannon mounted on a cart, used by the Hussites in the Hussite Wars of 1419–34, and called by them a *houfnice*. This became the *haubitze* in German and *houwitser* in Dutch. The howitzer in its modern sense of a mortar-cannon hybrid originated in the mid-17th century, possibly in Sweden. The word entered English usage in 1695 and by 1704 Marlborough had howitzers in his siege trains. Despite having a large caliber of 8 to 10 inches (20.3–25.4 cm), they were light enough to be drawn by six horses, as opposed to the 13 horses required for his 6-pounder cannon.

The reforms of Gribeauval in the 18th century (see page 96) saw a range of different caliber howitzers adopted by the French, and by this time the Prussian army was using 10- and 18-pounder howitzers. By the 1760s the Prussians had also adopted 7-pounder howitzers as "battalion guns," to provide fire support for infantry. With their short limbers the howitzers were mobile enough to be transported quickly around the battlefield, and powerful enough to lob shells over the heads of advancing infantry and beyond defensive breastworks.

In siege work the howitzer, more mobile than the mortar, could be repositioned to engage targets as opportunity arose — for example, to target defenders attempting to repair walls. By the 19th century a range of howitzer calibers could be used in concert. At the 1812 Siege of Badajoz, for instance, three different calibers were used: a small 5.5 inch to target defenders; heavy 24-pounders to bombard fortifications; and 12-pounders to provide covering fire during an assault on a breach in the fortifications.

Big and small

Howitzers continued to proliferate through the 19th century. Very light versions became "mountain howitzers"; for example, a cannon with a decent 12-pounder caliber but which weighed as little as 196 pounds (89 kg). They could be broken down into components and transported on a mule. A mountain howitzer on

"The action, so far as the artillery was concerned, soon became general. The duller sounds of the howitzers was joined to the sharp reports of the rifled cannon … The firing was deliberate, though not always accurate."

E.C. GORDON, CIVIL WAR HOWITZER GUNNER, WRITING TO HIS BROTHER IN 1861

wheels is claimed by some to have been the first wheeled vehicle to traverse North America when it was taken on an expedition in 1843.

The usefulness of howitzers was brought home to the British Army by the experiences of commanders in the Boer War in South Africa (1899–1903), where the Boers used them to good effect. In 1908 the British Army approved its own new howitzer: the 4.5-inch (11 cm), which would remain in service until the Second World War.

The onset of the First World War saw the development of truly monstrous guns. The most famous of these was the German railroad gun Big Bertha, which had a 17-inch (43 cm) caliber and fired shells weighing 1, 719 pounds (780 kg), each at a range of 9.3 miles (15 km). According to *British Military Operations: France and Belgium 1915*, these "traveled through the air with a noise like a runaway tramcar on badly laid rails." The name of the gun derived from the German Dicke Bertha — the gun was named after Bertha Krupp, heiress of the Krupp armaments firm. Four of these monsters were produced, initially with the goal of reducing the steel-clad forts set up by the Belgians, for instance around Liège, which were supposed to be invulnerable to artillery, but which were quickly smashed up by the great guns.

By the end of the war even bigger howitzers were being built. The British ordered a number of 18-inch (46 cm) howitzers, although they were not delivered until after the cessation of hostilities. One of them still survives (one of only 12 surviving railroad howitzers in the world). At 213 tons (190 tonnes) it weighs the same as about 17 school buses.

During the 20th century the howitzer continued to evolve into what is known as a gun-howitzer (an artillery piece closer to a direct-fire gun than a traditional howitzer), which remains a mainstay of modern armed forces. The US Marine Corps, for instance, uses the M777 Lightweight 155 mm howitzer because, as they explain, it "provides timely, accurate, and continuous firepower in support of Marine Infantry forces." The M777 was adopted precisely because it is light and "highly deployable," and can be towed by 7.8-ton (7-tonne) trucks or lifted by helicopters. Gun-howitzers are well suited to the demands of modern warfare in places like Afghanistan, where it is often necessary to strike at units over the crest of a hill as well as those in line of sight; a gun-howitzer can hit the forward slopes and the reverse ones.

The Howitzer

[A] Tube

[B] Recuperators

[C] Cradle

[D] Spade

[E] Bottom carriage

[F] Jacket

[G] Barrel (jacket and tube together)

KEY FEATURE:

THE SHELL

Howitzers were often loaded with exploding shells rather than normal shot. The explosive shell, an iron sphere filled with gunpowder and fitted with a burning fuse, was first used in 1588, by the Spanish besieging the Dutch fortress of Wachtendonck. Also used were metal cannonballs heated until red hot and then lobbed into a fortress to start fires. Today's howitzer shells can achieve amazing range and accuracy.

Howitzers are simply cannon that fire shells with high trajectories; as such they share the same features as other contemporary cannons, such as barrels, cradles, trunions, and carriages. The advent of breeches and pneumatic recoil systems made a great impact on the design and efficacy of howitzers, but arguably the most important element of a howitzer system is not part of the gun at all, but the ballistic tables that made "over the horizon" or non line of sight targeting possible.

24

Inventor(s):

Johann Nikolaus von Dreyse

NEEDLE GUN

Type:

Bolt-action breech-loading rifle

Social

Political

Tactical ■

Technical ■

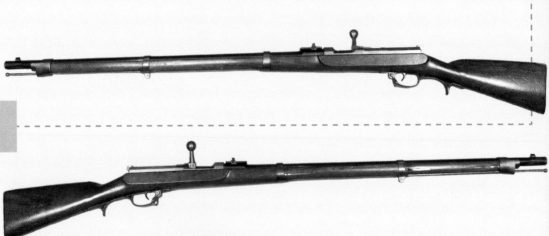

1836

The Dreyse "needle gun" or *Zündnadelgewehr* was primitive, dangerous, and obsolete within just a few years of its arrival, yet it also ranks as one of the most seminal firearms in history, profoundly affecting the development of modern warfare and ushering in a new and dreadful age of mass killing.

Triple threat

Its revolutionary qualities derived from being the first mass-produced, widely available gun to combine rifling, breech-loading, and cartridges. These developments answered the serious flaws that had bedeviled muskets since their arrival. Muzzle-loading limited the rate of fire achievable and the need to use a tamping rod meant that the gunner had to stand — exposed to enemy fire — to reload. With powder, shot, and primer all needing to be loaded separately, it was hardly surprising that loading was so slow. Muzzle-loading also meant the ball had to be relatively loose-fitting in the barrel, or it would be too hard to ram down; this in turn ruled out rifling the barrel and restricted muskets to smoothbores. Smoothbore guns were hopelessly inaccurate, and the loose-fitting balls meant that the explosive gases released when the powder detonated would leak around the sides of the ball in the barrel, wasting much of the propellant force.

To overcome these drawbacks it was necessary to develop a gun that loaded at the base of the barrel — via a gap or breech — with a cartridge, which included a ball that fit tightly into the rifled barrel. Such a gun could fire with far greater accuracy over a longer range, yet could also achieve much higher rates of fire and be reloaded from a prone position. The obvious attractions of this technology were countered by the technical difficulties in achieving it. A successful cartridge required a primer that would detonate instantly and powder that would burn evenly and quickly in one direction, and a rifled barrel was only practical if the gun could be breech-loaded. Yet it was breech-loading that was the hardest to perfect.

All of these technologies had been invented previously — two of them hundreds of years earlier. The first successful rifle (from the German word *riffeln*, to groove) was invented around 1700 but with a few exceptions (see page 92) was restricted to hunting weapons where the difficulties of loading were less important. By the mid-19th century rifles were achieving hitherto impossible feats of accuracy. In 1860 Queen Victoria opened a shooting competition by firing a new Whitworth rifle: she scored the most accurate shot in the history of the contest.

The earliest cartridges appeared in the 16th century, in the form of twists of paper that held the powder charge for a musket, and around 1600 the cartridge began to include the ball. By the end of the 17th century it was standard practice for the soldier to tear off the ball end of the cartridge with his teeth, pour in the powder charge, and then ram in the paper as a packing wad and the ball on top.

Breech-loading had been tried with artillery as early as the 14th century (see page 107). Leonardo da Vinci is said to have invented, in his Codex Atlanticus of 1500–10, the hackbut, a heavy matchlock musket with a barrel that unscrewed near the base for loading, known as a "turn-off" breech. Screw-plug breech-loaders, where the breech could be unsealed and sealed with a screw at the rear of the barrel, may have been invented as early as the 16th century, but the first truly successful military application was the rifle patented by Scotsman Captain Patrick Ferguson in 1776. In 1812 Swiss gunmaker Johannes Pauly invented a hinged-barrel breech-loading gun that used a paper cartridge, achieving a remarkable 22 shots in one minute in one demonstration. But this was a sporting gun — successful military application of the breech-loading and cartridge combination would have to wait for the needle gun.

Secret weapon

Pauly's staff at his Parisian gunsmiths' included the Prussian Johann Nikolaus von Dreyse. In 1836 he patented the world's first bolt-action breech-loader, introducing the system that would become standard for rifles used by all the armed forces of the world, and which is still used today in many hunting and target-shooting rifles. The breech is opened and then closed and locked with a bolt similar to that used for a door. The needle gun got its name from the slender, spring-loaded needle within the bolt. Drawing back the bolt simultaneously cocked the needle firing pin; pulling the trigger released the spring, which drove the needle forward, piercing the paper cartridge that was used to load the gun. The needle struck a disk of detonating material in the center of the cartridge, which set off the charge and fired a 0.6-inch (15.2 mm) caliber bullet up the rifled barrel. Thus, Dreyse's gun combined breech-loading, cartridges, and rifling.

The needle gun was far from perfect. The seal on the breech was not sufficiently tight enough to stop hot gases from the explosion from jetting out. The needle itself was fragile and broke easily, especially because it was exposed to corrosive gases from the igniting powder. The first versions of the gun could be

"No man can stand against that rapid fire."

quite dangerous. In one incident Dreyse turned up to a demonstration for the Prussian army with his arm swathed in bandages from an accident in which a bullet had exploded during loading. He was told to come back when he had improved his design.

Evidently he succeeded; in 1841 the Prussians adopted the needle gun as their standard-issue weapon. The top brass were excited by its potential: it could get off four or five rounds for every one fired from a muzzle-loaded musket and could be reloaded from a prone position. Initially, they tried to keep the weapon's core technology secret. It would take dramatic demonstrations of its powers to make the other European nations take notice.

Rapid fire

The first of these demonstrations came during a minor engagement in the Second Schleswig War of 1864, the Lundby skirmish. At the time, the acme of infantry tactics was deemed to be the "shock tactics" devised by the French, which was predicated on the essential uselessness of the musket volley. Accuracy was so low, and reloading so lengthy, that a charging unit could expect to contend with just a single, relatively harmless volley before closing with the enemy. Accordingly, the French had achieved great success by launching frenzied bayonet charges at their opponents. The Second Schleswig War pitted the Danes against the Austrians and the Prussians; the former two were still wedded to shock tactics, but when a Danish contingent charged a Prussian unit armed with needle guns at Lundby, they discovered that the rules of

infantry gunnery had radically changed. The Prussians were able to fire rapidly, while aiming, without breaking cover. The Danes were mowed down, losing half their men in just 20 minutes; the Prussians suffered three minor casualties.

Lundby should have put other nations on notice, but it was not until the Seven Weeks' War of 1866, between Prussia and Austria, that the lesson would be properly learned. Superior Prussian staff work, and command incompetence from the Austrians, saw them enveloped at Königgrätz (Sadowa) in 1866. The Austrian troops, armed with muzzle-loading weapons, launched brave frontal assaults but were horribly outgunned by the needlegun-armed Prussians.

In the space of seven weeks Prussia gained 5 million inhabitants and 25,000 square miles (65,000 km²) of territory. Churchill later wrote that "a premonitory shudder went through France." In the aftermath of the war, all the armies of Europe rushed to equip themselves with breech-loading rifles. The Swedes adopted the hagström, the Italians the carcano, and the French the chassepot. The latter gun in particular was far superior to the needle gun. The breech was more secure; the range, accuracy, and reliability greater; and the rate of fire higher. By the time of the Franco–Prussian War of 1870–71, just six years after the Second Schleswig War and four years after the Seven Weeks' War, the needle gun was obsolete; yet by then it had revolutionized warfare.

25

Inventor(s):

William Armstrong

BREECH-LOADING FIELD ARTILLERY

Type:

Artillery

Social

Political

Tactical ■

Technical ■

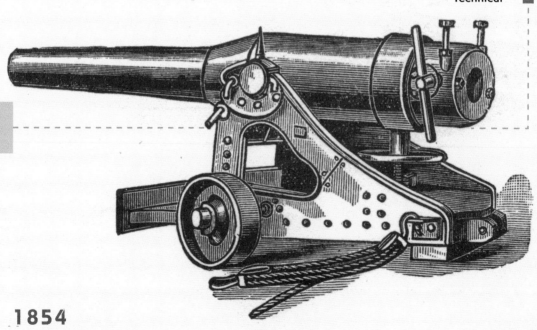

1854

The development of field artillery paralleled that of firearms, but the greater size and power of cannons posed greater technical problems, so that artillery lagged behind. From the mid-19th century, however, a range of innovations came together to create ever more powerful and rapid-firing cannons that would become the most lethal weapons of the age.

A problem of obturation

As with firearms, cannons suffered from the technical drawbacks of smoothbore, muzzle-loaded barrels. Breech-loading in combination with rifling promised more rapid fire with greater range and accuracy. Indeed, many of the earliest cannons had been breech-loading, with removable chambers that could be packed with powder and slotted into the breech, with wooden wedges banged in to hold the assemblage together. Typically known as a *perrier*, this kind of light breech-loading cannon was used in the Hundred Years' War. But with more powerful charges came the problem of insufficient obturation — the sealing of the breech to prevent venting of hot gases from the explosion of the charge. For several centuries only single-piece cast-metal guns could cope with the explosive pressures. Firearms such as the French chassepot would overcome the problem by using rubber obturating rings, but cannons would require something stronger.

Meanwhile, several other advances were changing the nature of cannons in the post-Napoleonic era. Rifling was introduced to improve accuracy, and wrought iron was introduced in place of cast iron. By the 1840s, wrought-iron guns were available that were superior to cast-iron ones, but militaries around the world resisted their introduction because of some high-profile cannon-burstings.

Application of scientific principles to the construction of guns saw the development of "built-up" guns. These were made by "shrinking" concentric tubes around the parts of the barrel subject to the greatest forces, resulting in bottle-shaped cannons. This was the method employed by William Armstrong, who in 1854 designed a built-up, breech-loaded, rifled cannon. His was not the first such cannon — combined rifling and breech-loading had been achieved by Cavelli in Italy in 1846, whereas in England Joseph Whitworth's 3-pounder could achieve astonishing accuracy at distances of over 7,000 yards (6,400 m). But Armstrong's was the most successful and the first widely adopted for field and naval artillery. In his version, the breech was at the rear and was closed with a vent-piece of steel, dropped into a slot and secured with a screw. Two years later the

The shattered remnants of Bazeilles, a village guarding the approaches to Sedan, where Prussian breech-loading field artillery would crush the French army.

showed off a cast-steel 3-pounder that was much lighter than previous weapons. But fears that steel would prove dangerously brittle led to suspicion from famously conservative ordnance overseers in many nations.

Both Krupp's and Armstrong's guns used a soft metal ring for obturation, but in the case of the latter the seal was not strong enough to cope with larger charges. In addition, the longer, cylindrical shells required by rifled cannons were heavier than the spherical balls used by smoothbore cannons, so that in some of these early rifled breech-loaders the muzzle velocity of the shell was lower than in the contemporary muzzle-loaders. Because impact energy is determined by the mass of the projectile multiplied by the square of the velocity, the speed of a projectile is much more important than its mass. Over a longer trajectory, the heavier and more aerodynamic rifled cannon shells retained their velocity much better than spherical shot, but over short distances muzzle-loading balls could offer a greater impact. Accordingly, the British actually went back to smoothbore artillery for a while.

Technological advances continued apace. The interrupted screw breech was an ingenious solution to the problem of closing a breech quickly. The rear of the bore was screw-threaded, as was the plug used to seal it. But instead of having to screw the plug all the way in with

German cannonmaker Alfred Krupp devised a different breech-loaded, rifled cannon — his was made of steel.

Guns of steel

Cast steel offered twice the tensile strength of wrought iron and four times that of cast iron. Steel had been known since the Iron Age but since its chemistry was not understood its creation had been haphazard and rare. German gunmaker and inventor Friedrich Krupp mastered the art of making cast steel, and his son Alfred came to be known as the Cannon King. In 1851, at the Great Exhibition in London, he

" ... one looked in vain for a single intact, undamaged corpse; the men had been mutilated by the fire ..."

PRUSSIAN OBSERVER AT THE BATTLE OF SEDAN (1871)

repeated turns, segments of the threads on each element were removed so that the plug, mounted on hinges, could swing all the way in and then be secured with just part of a single turn, all of its threads engaging at once. Obturation was provided by the mushroom vent-bolt, devised by French officer Charles Ragon de Bange. Krupp's guns used a different system, with a sliding breechblock and a metallic cartridge. When the charge in the cartridge detonated, the brass case expanded against the walls of the bore and formed an obturating seal. Breech-loaded rifled cannons had come of age and were adopted by the Prussians in 1861, the Russians in 1867, and the USA in 1870.

In the chamber pot

The French had their own version, but this was to prove hopelessly inferior to the steel Krupp guns with which the Prussians were equipped. The gap was exposed at the Battle of Sedan, the climax of the Franco–Prussian War in 1871, and the battle where field artillery regained the primacy it had last enjoyed in the Napoleonic era. Bottled up in the town of Sedan, ringed by hills on which were sited 500 Krupp guns, the French army was blown to pieces. When he saw the situation, the French general Ducrot famously observed, "We are in the chamber pot and about to be shat upon."

Another technical challenge facing artillery was the problem of recoil. A typical large smoothbore cannon could roll back up to 6.6 feet (2 m) on firing, which meant that it had to be "relaid" every time it was fired. This in turn meant re-aiming. The problem was solved by developing mechanisms that absorbed and stored the recoil energy and then used it to push the cannon back into position.

The final piece in the jigsaw was the development of new smokeless powders which offered slower, more controlled burning. This in turn meant that the explosive burning was spread more evenly along the length of the bore, resulting in less extreme pressures at any one point, yet greater force and muzzle velocity. It was now possible to build longer, larger-bore guns without the breech having to be made unmanageably thick.

In 1897 all these advances came together in a single gun: the French *soixante-quinze*, or 2.95 inch (75 mm) M1897. With a hydro-pneumatic recoil mechanism, rapid-loading interrupted-screw breech-loading system and "fixed" (i.e., all-in-one) shells, it could fire 15 shells a minute and get them all on target. Twenty years later, this was still widely regarded as the best artillery gun in the world, and was adopted by the US as well as the French. It and similar guns developed by the Germans and Russians would see the proportion of battlefield deaths caused by artillery fire, which had been running at 60 percent in the Napoleonic era, leap from just 2.5 percent in the 1877–88 Russo-Turkish war, back to 60 percent on the Western Front in the First World War.

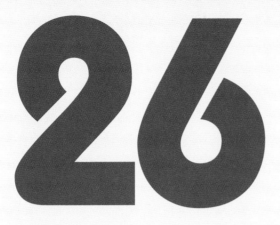

26

Inventor(s):

Richard Jordan Gatling

GATLING GUN

Type:

Rapid-repeating firearm

Social

Political

Tactical

Technical

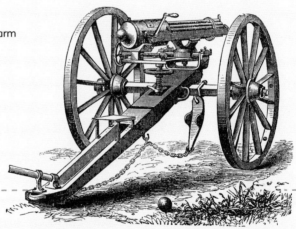

"It occurred to me that if I could invent a machine — a gun — which could, by rapidity of fire, enable one man to do as much battle duty as a hundred, that it would, to a great extent, supersede the necessity of large armies."

1861 RICHARD GATLING, 1877

As the American Civil War raged, Richard Jordan Gatling, from Money's Neck, North Carolina, developed a field weapon that was to become symbolic of the changing nature of warfare in the industrial era. The weapon consisted of six barrels mounted in a revolving cylinder. Not adopted by the US Army until 1866, the first purchases (12 for $1,000 each) were made by Union Major-General Benjamin Butler in 1864; in the following years, it was purchased by most European governments.

Richard Jordan Gatling

Rapid Fire

The American Civil War (1861–65) had done much to illustrate the changes wrought on warfare by the industrial revolution. Improved communications encouraged a fluid corps-based offensive posture that was countered by defensive technologies such as trench networks and barbed wire. Although not widely used during the Civil War, the Gatling gun nevertheless contributed to this development by allowing a limited number of combatants to produce a withering intensity of firepower.

Though the Gatling gun was, after initial development phases, reasonably reliable, it lacked ease of mobility over difficult terrain. This may have been one reason why George Armstrong Custer did not take the available Gatling batteries with him as he set off toward the Little Big Horn River valley. How different the outcome might have been if his command had possessed the formidable firepower of the Gatling gun. But perhaps the most decisive use of the gun came in 1898, during the Spanish–American War. At the Battle of Bloody Ford, the Gatling gun detachment of the Fifth Army Corps was able to fire as many as 18,000 rounds

in under 10 minutes, turning the tide of the battle and saving many American lives.

By that stage the Gatling gun was already in decline. The invention of the automatic Maxim gun (see page 112) had superseded the Gatling and orders were dwindling. Its inventor died in 1903, and the weapon was obsolete within 10 years. However, as an innovation, the Gatling gun established the supremacy of industrial nations. It enhanced the ability of colonial armies to offset the disadvantages of limited manpower through the advantage of enhanced firepower. The Gatling gun and its immediate predecessors were at their most effective in pre-prepared emplacements, where the risk of being outflanked was greatly reduced, and interlocking fields of fire further improved the killing capacity of each weapon. This shift in favor of a defensive and static posture was to contribute significantly to the entrenched killing fields of Flanders.

27

Inventor(s):
Hiram Maxim

MAXIM MACHINE GUN

Social ■

Political

Tactical ■

Technical

Type:

Heavy machine gun

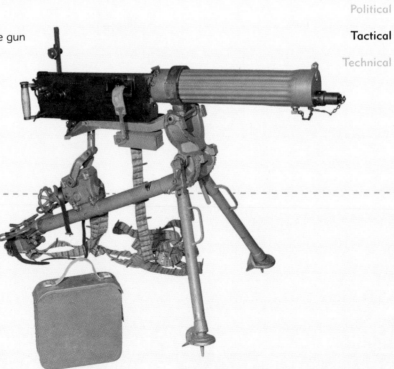

1884

In 1885 Hiram Maxim invented the first fully automatic machine gun — a firearm that fired, expelled the empty case, chambered the next round, and fired again, and continued to do so indefinitely as long as the trigger was depressed and the ammunition continued to be fed in. In doing so, he had put into one man's hands the firepower of 40 riflemen. An expert rifleman could fire 15 shots in a minute; a machine-gunner could fire 600 shots a minute. Few military minds could grasp how the nature of battle had changed, a failure that was to have horrific consequences.

Hiram Maxim

The missed opportunity of the mitrailleuse

There had been experiments with repeaters and multiple-shot weapons since early in the history of firearms, but the first practical machine gun was the French *mitrailleuse*, developed between 1851 and 1869 by the Belgians Faschamp and Montigny, under the patronage of Napoleon III (a keen student of gun technology). Originally equipped with 37 barrels (later reduced to 25), it weighed a ton and was mounted on a carriage pulled by a team of four horses. In one minute — or longer, depending on how quickly it was cranked — it could fire 370 shots (10 magazines). Here was a weapon with the potential to transform warfare, but unfortunately the French did not appreciate what they had, conceiving of the *mitrailleuse* as an artillery weapon, to be stationed not with the infantry but with the cannons. What's more, in a ham-fisted attempt at secrecy the French successfully prevented most of their own men from becoming familiar enough with the gun to operate it to full effect, but failed to prevent Prussians from discovering its existence. Stationed with the artillery, the *mitrailleuse*

units were easy prey during the Franco–Prussian War for the Prussian artillery batteries, which concentrated their fire specifically to destroy them. On one occasion when a single *mitrailleuse was* used as an infantry support weapon at the Battle of Gravelotte, it accounted for over 2,600 Prussian casualties: about half of the enemy troops. The French failed to pick up on the lessons offered by their experience of the *mitrailleuse*, but the Prussians were more attentive (see below).

Something for the Europeans

At this point Hiram Maxim enters the story. Born in the USA of French stock, Maxim was an inventor who had worked in the electrical industry; he invented a better mousetrap and the world's first automatic fire sprinkler. On a business trip to Europe he was advised by another American, "If you really want to make a pile of money, invent something that will enable these Europeans to cut each other's throats with greater facility." The idea for the "something" came to him when he got a sore shoulder from

MAXIM MACHINE GUN

the recoil after firing a gun; the force of the recoil could be put to good use, he reasoned, and in 1883–84 he came up with a fully automated gun that used the power of the recoil to open the breech, eject the spent cartridge case, and chamber a new one. With his new gun able to fire over 600 rounds in a minute, the barrel inevitably became extremely hot so he equipped it with a cooling jacket filled with oil (later changed to water). Cartridges were fed in via a canvas ammunition belt.

The new device astonished observers and was rapidly adopted by the Europeans, as foretold. It helped that Maxim was an inveterate self-promoter. He moved to Britain, became a citizen, cultivated contacts with royalty, and was duly rewarded with a knighthood in 1901. The Maxim machine gun was adopted by the British Army in 1889, the Royal Navy in 1892, the Germans in 1899, and also the Russians.

The devastating impact of the new weapon was felt in conflicts from Kamchatka to the Sudan. The British used it in colonial wars including the Gambia (1887), the Matabele War of 1893–94, the Chitral campaign on the Northwest Frontier in 1895, and the suppression of the Mahdi's revolt at Omdurman in the Sudan in 1898. In the Second Boer War (1899–1902) both sides had Maxim machine guns and the British fared rather less well. Satirist Hilaire Belloc reflected on the importance of the gun to the colonial project in his poem "The Modern Traveler": "Whatever happens, we have got/The Maxim Gun, and they have not."

War of the machines

The onset of the First World War saw both the British and the Germans armed with versions of the Maxim machine gun. In Britain Maxim, having refined his design to make it simpler to maintain on the battlefield, went into partnership with the arms firm Vickers. In 1912 the British army adopted the Vickers Maxim heavy machine gun. Although relatively slow-firing, at 500 rpm, and heavy, weighing 83.1 pounds (37.7 kg) with its tripod, it was to prove its worth in the First World War. In August 1916, for instance, during the Battle of the Somme, the 10 Vickers of the 100th Machine Gun Company kept up 12 straight hours of machine-gun fire, pouring almost a million rounds into a patch of ground 1,969 yards (1,800 m) away, and going through 100 barrels. None of the guns broke down.

By this time the British had already suffered much worse at the hands of the German version of the Maxim, the LMG 08/15, known as the Spandau after the name of one of the Imperial arsenals. German units were well equipped with the weapons, with six machine guns per battalion. The French, by contrast, had just two machine guns per battalion. Their commanders still clung to the outmoded, mid-19th century tactics of *l'offensive brutale et à outrance* (brutal and extreme attacks). But it was the new reality of warfare that was brutal, with the machine gun as its totemic weapon. Winston Churchill characterized the new era: "War, which used to be cruel and magnificent, has now become cruel and squalid."

The Maxim Machine Gun

A 1904 model Maxim machine gun consisted of around 150 component parts for the gun itself, dozens more for the steam-condensing device that was fitted to the water jacket, and over 80 more components for the tripod.

[A] Receiver
[B] Corrugated water-cooling jacket
[C] Tripod
[D] Barrel
[E] Spade grips

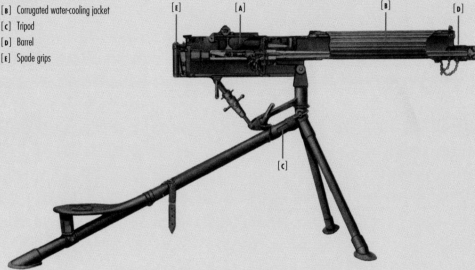

KEY FEATURE:
WATER-COOLING JACKET

Rapid fire would heat the barrel until it deformed and fractured, so Maxim machine guns relied on water-cooling jackets through which water was pumped around the barrel. The water in the jacket had to be passed through a condenser to cool it, but would still need to be replaced around every 750 rounds.

"The machine-gunner is best thought of as a sort of machine-minder, whose principal task was to feed ammunition belts into the breech ... "

JOHN KEEGAN, *THE FACE OF BATTLE* (2004)

28

Inventor(s):

Royal Small Arms Factory

SHORT MAGAZINE LEE-ENFIELD

Type:

Firearm

Social

Political

Tactical ■

Technical ■

1903

The Short Magazine Lee-Enfield, aka the SMLE or "smellie," was one of the most widely produced and probably longest-lived bolt-action rifles of the 20th century. It served as the primary infantry weapon of the British and their Imperial/Commonwealth territories in both world wars, and its combination of speed and sturdiness led to its being widely regarded as the best bolt-action rifle of the lot.

Magazines

The needle gun and chassepot were single-shot weapons — each bullet had to be loaded individually. The next step in the evolution of the rifle to produce ever more rapid fire was the introduction of magazines, which could hold multiple bullets to speed up loading greatly. One of the first magazine-fed rifles was the Vetterli adopted by the Swiss Army in 1868, which had a tubular magazine under the barrel. A similar magazine was introduced by German gunmaker Peter Paul Mauser in 1884, with an 8-round tubular magazine. The French Modèle 1886, used in the French Army until 1940, also had a tubular magazine.

But tubular magazines were unsatisfactory. When fully loaded they ruined the balance of the rifle by making it front-heavy, and the arrangement of the bullets, with the tip of one resting against the one in front's base (where the primer was stored), made it dangerous. In 1885 Austrian gunmaker Ferdinand Mannlicher introduced a magazine where five bullets were stacked vertically in a clip, and in 1893 Mauser did away with the clip. Where the Mannlicher required the rifleman to cycle through all five

bullets and then replace the clip, Mauser's rifle was charged with the rounds but not the clip. Extra rounds could then be loaded individually to top up the stack in the heat of battle.

In 1888 the British Army adopted the magazine-fed Lee-Metford bolt-action rifle as its standard service rifle; the magazine and bolt action were designed by James Paris Lee, an expat Canadian turned American, whereas the barrel with its rifling was made by William Metford. But the Metford rifling had been designed for black powder charges, and the adoption of cordite, the British version of Charles Nobel's new smokeless explosive, which burned hotter, meant that the Royal Small Arms Factory in Enfield, London, had to devise a new, deeper rifling to cope. The result was the Lee-Enfield Mark I rifle, introduced in 1895.

One smellie for all

This rifle would evolve into the SMLE, as a result of British experiences in the Boer War (1899–1902), which convinced the military that a shorter rifle that could function as a carbine

" ... a consistently satisfactory standard of accuracy under service conditions. "

"SMLE," *BRITISH TEXTBOOK OF SMALL ARMS*, 1929

A British soldier shelters in a trench during the Battle of the Somme, his "smellie" poised for action with bayonet fixed.

(a shorter, lighter rifle used by the cavalry and artillery) was needed, so that a "one-size-fits-all" model could be used for everyone. This would simplify the logistics of manufacture and parts. Accordingly, in 1903 the SMLE appeared, properly known as the ".303 Rifle, Short, Magazine, Lee-Enfield, Mark I." The punctuation makes clear that it is not the magazine that is short, but the rifle itself — where the Lee-Metford had been 49.5 inches (1,257 mm), the SMLE was 44.57 inches (1,132 mm). In 1907 the Mark III SMLE was introduced, and this would be the model used in the First World War.

Experts roundly condemned the rifle/carbine hybrid and predicted disaster, but in fact the SMLE turned out to be one of the great triumphs of military engineering. Crucially, it could produce more rapid fire than any of its competitors. This chimed well with the newfound British emphasis on combining speed with accuracy. Having learned from the Boer War the importance of marksmanship, the British instituted a program of training for their infantry, with an annual weapons test where soldiers had to demonstrate deliberate, snap, and rapid-fire practice, with ranges up to 600 yards (549 m). The test included the "mad minute," in which the soldier had to fire 15 rounds at a target 300 yards (274 m) away; most of the men successfully landed all their shots within a 2-foot (0.6 m) circle. In the 1930s an instructor at the British Small Arms School Corps set a record of firing 37 rounds in a minute. The fruits of this labor would be felt at the Battle of Mons in August 1914, when the German troops came up against the professional soldiers of the British Expeditionary Force, who laid down such rapid fire with their SMLEs that the German commander, General von Kluck, believed he was facing machine guns.

Lieutenant RA Macleod of the 80th Battalion XV Brigade, Royal Field Artillery, recalled:

> Our Infantry were splendid; they had only scratchings in the ground made with their entrenching tools, which didn't give much cover, but they stuck it out and returned a good rate of fire. The German Infantry fired from the hip as they advanced but their fire was very inaccurate.

In fact, the lessons of the high-volume fire produced by modern rifles had been available as early as 1870, when the Prussians launching frontal assaults on French troops armed with the chassepot had been cut down en masse. Rapid fire gave a decisive advantage to the defender; frontal assault was now suicidal, and all the old tactics of columns or squares of troops became obsolete. Mobile skirmishing, where small units advanced by rushes under covering fire, was the new order of the day; a lesson that the Prussians absorbed in the Franco–Prussian War, but which was promptly forgotten by many (most notably the British) until after the carnage of the First World War.

Soldier-proof

The SMLE's success was due mainly to the two components designed by Lee. The magazine, which held 10 bullets, was larger than those of competitor rifles and the bolt pull was notably shorter than others. It had a rear-locking bolt, which meant that the bolt had far less to travel than those with front lug designs, and this, combined with the smooth internal machining, made the bolt action fast and easy. Other features of the SMLE included its walnut forestock, which extended all the way up to the muzzle, and its distinctively profiled butt stock, featuring a semi-pistol grip and a steel butt plate with a trapdoor and a compartment for tools and cleaning equipment. Its robust and relatively simple design meant that it stood up well to the rigors and dirt of trench warfare, and it was considered the most "soldier-proof" bolt-action rifle available.

The rifle did have some deficiencies. For instance, its rimmed ammunition packed less punch than the German or American standard-issue bullets, although it was perfectly adequate to stop an oncoming soldier. The bolts for the rifles were not interchangeable. Overall, the German Mauser rifles were considered to offer higher performance and engineering, but the advantages of the SMLE meant that it remained in service for over 60 years as a frontline weapon and, for training and sniper duties, into the 1980s. At least 5 million SMLEs were made in the 20th century, by factories as far afield as India, Australia, and the USA. Not only did the "smellie" help to check the rapid German advance at the start of the First World War before going on to give stout service through the Second World War and the Korean conflict; it also helped the Afghans to defeat the Soviets in the 1980s, and remains in service in South Asia.

Afghan soldier with SMLE in 1985, demonstrating the longevity of the Lee-Enfield.

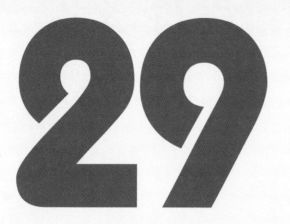

29

Inventor(s):

Isaac Newton Lewis

LEWIS GUN

Social

Political

Tactical

Technical

Type:

Light machine gun

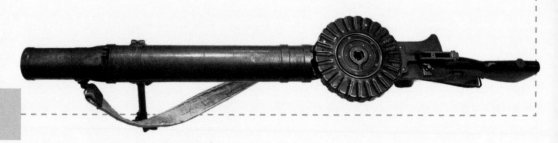

"The Lewis Gun resembles a submarine. It does its work best by popping up when and where it is least expected and delivering a smashing blow in a trice."

THE COMPLETE LEWIS GUNNER, BY AN INSTRUCTOR, 1941

1911

The heavy machine gun in the Maxim mold had transformed the First World War battlefields into nightmarish stalemates. But guns like these were restricted in their tactical applications. They were extremely heavy, requiring tripods and reasonable amounts of space to set up, and teams of several men to operate them. Troops could not move them quickly across battlefields, limiting the mobility and responsiveness of units. A light machine gun was needed. This role was fulfilled by the Lewis machine gun, the distinctive outline of which would become a major feature of the war.

I. N. Lewis

Gas power

Recoil, the power source for Maxim's automatic mechanism, was not the only way of powering a gun. One alternative was to harness the pressure of the hot gases created when the powder charge exploded. Gas-operated firearms were pioneered by the great American gunmaker John M. Browning. He invented the technology in 1889, and it was perfected by Colt in 1895 to produce the Colt–Browning machine gun (see page 142). This was air-cooled, saving weight on the water jacket used by the Maxim. The same year Hotchkiss perfected a gas-operated design originated by Captain Baron Adolf Odkolek von Augeza of Austria, in which the combustion gases were tapped from a port in the barrel to drive a piston, which pushed back the bolt, expending the spent cartridge. The piston also compressed a spring, which then rebounded, closing the bolt and loading a new round. A similar system would be used for the Lewis gun, and like the Hotchkiss it too would be air-cooled.

In 1911, based on an earlier design by Dr. Samuel McLean, Colonel Isaac Newton Lewis created his light, air-cooled, gas-powered machine gun. Weighing just 26 pounds

(11.8 kg), it had a distinctive shroud around the barrel that narrowed slightly toward the muzzle, and an equally distinctive top-mounted circular pan magazine (initially for 47 rounds). Unable to sell it to the US Army, in 1913 Lewis resigned his commission and set sail for Europe, which, as Maxim had proved, was hungry for "new ways to cut throats." Lewis' design was eagerly picked up by both the Belgians and the British, who were arming themselves against the gathering threat of war.

Automatic ad infinitum

In a Lewis gun, as in the Hotchkiss gun, combustion gases are harnessed to drive back a piston-rod, together with its attached bolt; on the underside of the piston-rod are teeth on a rack that drive a pinion to wind the spring and build tension. According to *The Complete Lewis Gunner*: "This tension now carries the piston-rod and bolt forward. The gas and return spring continue the backward and forward movement of the piston and bolt — alternately — thus giving us the automatic action *ad infinitum*."

Australian soldiers taking pot shots at enemy aircraft with a Lewis gun, toward the end of the First World War.

The gun is cooled by the action of the powder gases rushing out of the barrel, which are funneled in such a way as to expel the air from the radiator casing, creating a partial vacuum that draws in cold air through the vents in the rear to take the place of hot air expelled from the front. This cool air circulates freely along the 17 longitudinal aluminum fins sprung onto the barrel.

Although it was not especially cheap, it was fast to manufacture: six Lewis guns could be made in the time taken to build a single Vickers Maxim. This robust, simple, and above all mobile gun promised to enable a new, more mobile style of fighting to help break the stasis imposed by the tyranny of the heavy machine gun. "The Lewis Gun can be used with great effect in the attack and in open fighting," wrote "The Instructor" who authored the 1941 Lewis gun manual.

The Belgian rattlesnake

By 1916 over 50,000 Lewis guns had been made. By 1917, every British Army infantry section was issued with one, with 46 guns to a battalion, although the Belgian connection led to the German nickname of the weapon: "the Belgian rattlesnake," a reference to its distinctive sound. Its light weight saw it adopted by other services: Lewis guns were mounted on motorcycle sidecars and Royal Navy boats and it was the first machine gun to be fired from an airplane, becoming popular as a rear-mounted gun for observers. On a plane it could be mounted without its cooling jacket and radiator vanes, making it lighter still.

By the end of the First World War a 97-round magazine had increased the firepower of the Lewis gun, and it was widely used in various countries. At the outbreak of the Second World War many Lewis guns remained serviceable, and it was issued to Home Guard units in case of possible invasion of Britain.

The Lewis Gun

[A] Radiator shroud
[B] Barrel
[C] Drum magazine
[D] Rear sight
[E] Receiver

The 1941 manual *The Complete Lewis Gunner* expounded the many virtues of the gun, which included "Its mobility ... it can easily be maneuvered by one man ... Its Great Simplicity. Consists of only sixty-two parts ... Its cooling system is very simple, and requires no attention or water. It is well protected, very strong, and is not likely to be damaged in moving. The gun can be 'fed' in any position, and has hardly any 'kick' or recoil, etc, and is easy to handle."

[B] [A] [D]

[C] [E]

KEY FEATURE:
DRUM MAGAZINE

Along with the barrel shroud, the Lewis gun owes its distinctive profile to the drum magazine with which it was often fitted. This was very reliable, since it did not rely on an internal spring for ammo-feeding like most magazines, but made ingenious use of the gun's automatic mechanism to collect rounds.

30

Inventor(s):
The Chinese

Inventor(s):
The Chinese

HAND GRENADE

Type:

Explosive device

Social ■

Political

Tactical ■

Technical

1913

Hand grenades were among the earliest gunpowder devices, but steadily declined in importance from medieval to modern times. The advent of trench warfare in the early 20th century produced a radical reversal in the fortunes of this relatively low-tech weapon, and it became one of the most important tools in the infantry soldier's armory — personal artillery available to the meanest "grunt."

The earliest depiction of a grenade, from a 10th-century Buddhist manuscript.

Pomegranates with punch

Some of the first gunpowder weapons in medieval China were essentially hand grenades: segments of bamboo filled with black powder. In the Song Dynasty (960–1279 CE) proper hand grenades first appear. The *Wujing Zongyao* (Collection of the Most Important Military Techniques), a military manual from 1044 CE, includes discussion and illustrations of bombs consisting of balls of clay or iron packed with gunpowder and lit with a fuse to be hurled to explode and fragment on impact. Some were packed with charcoal or scrap metal for extra fragmentation.

Grenade technology spread along with other gunpowder weapons, via the Islamic world to Europe. Grenades were an important and useful part of siege warfare, typically used by sappers — the engineers concerned with digging the mines and trenches essential to the siege process. They could be tossed over walls and used to clear defenders, especially in confined spaces. Around this time the device got its name *granada*, "pomegranate," from Spanish via Middle French. The name refers to the way that the ball-shaped bombs were packed

with seedlike grains of corned powder, or musket balls packed in powder, as shown in an illustration in the 1620 manual *La Pyrotechnie*.

Early grenades weighed 1.5 to 3 pounds (0.68–1.36 kg), and were extremely dangerous to the user because of the risk of accidental detonation and the exposure to enemy fire entailed in standing still to light and throw them. For this reason, hurling them on the battlefield was a job for the strongest, tallest (and thus longest-limbed), and most reckless soldiers, with the result that grenadiers were the elite amongst infantrymen. This status was formalized by the end of the 17th century; in 1667 in France, for instance, each company had four grenadiers and four years later each battalion had one grenadier company. Other European nations followed suit. Grenadiers were distinguished by their brimless caps, unlike the wide-brimmed hats of most soldiers, so as not to interfere with their overarm throwing action. In the time of Frederick the Great and later Napoleon, the grenadiers formed elite divisions within the army, although by this

HAND GRENADE

time the actual grenades had been largely dispensed with; grenadiers were simply the biggest, most impressive soldiers, encouraged to grow fierce mustaches. To exaggerate their height, the brimless hats became distinctive, tall miter-style hats, and even the bearskin hats later introduced to the British Army by the Grenadier Guards. In the Second World War the German *Panzergrenadieren* were elite troops attached to tank units.

Decline and rise

With the decline in importance of siege warfare, the grenade also became less significant, although new designs arose. In the American Civil War, for instance, the Ketchum grenade had an oblong shape with an impact-percussion fuse at the top and a finned tail for stabilization. In the Russo-Japanese War of 1904–5, which foreshadowed so many themes of the First World War, grenades proved important. Once the First World War ossified into what was essentially one enormous siege, grenades once again took center stage. Initially, frontline troops improvised their own grenades, fixing high explosives fitted with a fuse (which had to be lit with a match) to a wooden handle and wrapping it in wire for fragmentation.

A Ketchum grenade with a percussion detonator, but missing its fins.

The British achieved a modest technological advance in 1915 with the jam tin grenade: a tin can stuffed with guncotton and metal scraps or even stones.

The troops were forced to improvise because of the failure of top brass to marshal adequate supplies of grenades. At the outbreak of war the British had only one type of grenade available: the expensive Mark I grenade, possessed in very limited numbers only by the Royal Engineers. The French were similarly ill-equipped, but the Germans slightly better so: they had about 170,000 grenades — mainly an impact-detonated "discus" bomb and the Model 1913 Kugel grenade. In late 1914, Sir John French estimated that the demand for hand grenades in the British forces was 4,000 per week. In November the supply was a laughable 70 per week, rising to 2,500 in December. Yet by the start of January demand had leapt to 10,000 per week, estimated to increase to 50,000 per day when the vast new armies being mobilized finished training and took to the field.

In the confines of trench warfare, the grenade was immensely useful; it could clear trenches and bunkers, putting the power of an artillery strike in the hands of the individual.

"A [grenade] inflicts terrible wounds. I never saw anything worse in the succeeding years of war."

LT P. NEAME, ROYAL ENGINEERS, AT THE BATTLE OF NEUVE CHAPELLE, 1915

The (almost) fatal flask

A grenade played a part in starting the First World War. Nedjelko Čabrinović was one of the men involved in the assassination of Archduke Franz Ferdinand; on July 28th, 1914, as the car bearing the Austrian prince approached, Cabrinovic was seen to take from his pocket what looked like a flask of whiskey, unscrew the top, and bash it against a lamp-post. There was a pop and he threw it at the Archduke, who deflected it with his arm. It landed on the ground and exploded, for it was a Serbian hand grenade; the "screw top" was a percussion cap, and it was activated by striking it against a hard surface.

Pineapples and potato mashers

The First World War saw the development of the two most iconic grenade shapes: the pineapple, introduced with the British No. 36 Mills bomb, and also used in the American M2; and the potato-masher stick grenade, in the form of the German *Stielhandgranate* 24. All had the same basic form, with a body, filler (explosive), and fuse. The body usually provides the fragmentation; the distinctive shape of pineapple grenades is the result of deep grooves in the metal casing to help with fragmentation on detonation. The No. 36 and the M2 both had a ringed safety pin that held down a handle known as "the spoon." When this was released, a spring striker hit the percussion cap, lighting the fuse. The potato masher was set off by pulling a porcelain bead located behind a metal cap at the end of the handle. Generally it was packed with TNT to give a bursting charge and produce a blast effect rather than fragmentation,

"A package for Hitler." A US infantryman trains with an M2 grenade during the Second World War.

although it could be fitted with a metal sleeve to achieve this.

Because the blast radius is usually greater than the throwing distance achievable, hand grenades have to be tossed from cover, or fused to allow the thrower to take cover. The need to throw grenades farther led to the development of a number of devices to project them from a rifle, such as rodded rifle bombs. These were grenades attached to a rod that fitted into the barrel of a rifle, which was loaded with a special blank, but the recoil was so heavy that the user was advised to put the butt against the ground for firing.

HAND GRENADE

31

Inventor(s):

The Ancient Greeks?

POISON GAS

Type:
Chemical weapon

Social
Political
Tactical
Technical

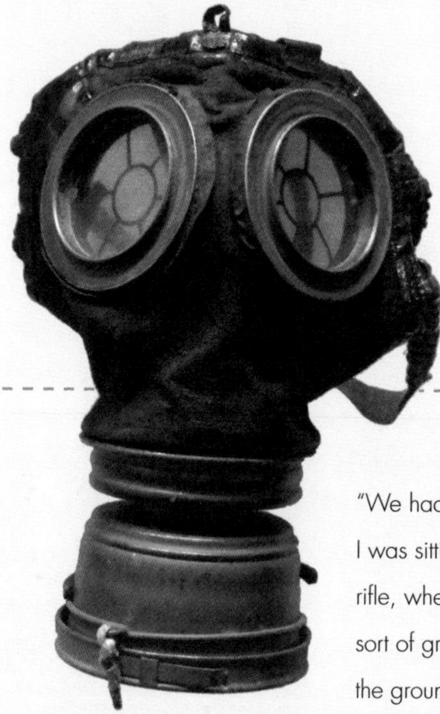

"We had a new man at the periscope … I was sitting on the fire step, cleaning my rifle, when he called out to me: 'There's a sort of greenish, yellow cloud rolling along the ground out in front, it's coming …'"

ARTHUR EMPEY, *NO MAN'S LAND*, 1917

1915

Poison gas is indelibly associated with the First World War, emblematic of the nightmare world of the trenches and the new depths of inhumanity achieved. Although it had limited impact in military terms, its psychological and cultural impact was profound and enduring.

Ancient sulfur

Use of poison gas dates back to ancient times. During the Second Peloponnesian War, c. 430 BCE, the Spartans are said to have burned a mixture of sulfur and charcoal to create toxic gas. Later in the same war, at the Siege of Delium in 424 BCE, the Boethians supposedly launched a gas attack against the Athenians, using a bellows to blow sulfur fumes and drive a primitive flame-thrower. Thucydides relates how they "fastened a huge cauldron to one end of a hollow wooden tube … In the cauldron they placed charcoal and sulfur, while to the other end of the tube they tied bellows … the charcoal and the sulfur … were fanned into a great blaze …"

In around 256 CE, in what is now Syria, the Roman fort Dura-Europas, known as "the Pompeii of the Syrian Desert," fell to an attack by Sassanian Persians. Archaeologist Simon James found yellow sulfur crystals around a pile of Roman bodies at the site, and was moved to reexamine the excavation archive to uncover what he describes as "one unrecognized deadly secret: the Roman soldiers who perished there

had not, as Robert du Mesnil du Buisson (the original excavator) believed, died by the sword or by fire but had been deliberately gassed by the Sassanian attacker."

In medieval China, the *Wujing Zongyao*, a military manual from 1044 CE, gives the formula for a gas bomb, which could include poison. Like grenades (see page 124), it would have been used in the mining and counter-mining aspects of siege warfare.

The king of war gases

In modern times there were various efforts to resurrect poison gas, but until the First World War they were quashed. In 1855 at the Siege of Sevastopol, for instance, Admiral Lord Dundonald drew up plans for a gas attack on the Russian forts using 448 tons (400 tonnes) of sulfur and 2,240 tons (2,000 tonnes) of coke, but was refused permission, and during the American Civil War (1861–65), John W. Doughty worked out a plan for using chlorine gas but the Secretary of War, Stanton, would not countenance it. In fact, the use of poisonous

William H. Livens with the projector (essentially a mortar) he devised to hurl drums of flammable oil; it was later adapted for poison-gas drums.

intelligence warning of the peril but discounted it, and the attack succeeded in breaking two Allied divisions. Cylinders released 201 tons (180 tonnes) of chlorine gas across a 3.7 mile (6 km) wide front; the cloud spread over French Territorial and Algerian forces, causing panic and terror. However, the Germans were unprepared for the success of their attack and did not have the reserves to exploit it.

Initially, the best response to the new threat that the appalled Allies could muster was to cover their noses and mouths with cotton soaked in water, urine, or bicarbonate of soda, but gas mask technology improved thereafter. Five months later the British responded with their own gas attack at Loos. Other gases used in the First World War included diphosgene, phosgene, chloropicrin, hydrocyanic acid (a nerve agent), and mustard gas, which caused festering sores on the skin and mucous membranes.

Mustard gas, known as the "king of war gases," was particularly hated because of its vile effects (including blindness), persistence, and ability to penetrate clothes. The first use of mustard gas was on the Eastern Front. When British troops were first exposed to it in July 1917, it caused 15,000 casualties, leading to 450 deaths.

Overall, some 138,880 tons (124,000 tonnes) of toxic agents were used during the war, causing 1.3 million casualties, or 4.6 percent of the total number, and of these casualties, 91,000 died. Only rarely did the use of chemical weapons achieve significant effects; at Ypres where its deployment had been such a

weaponry was specifically forbidden by the Hague Declaration and Convention of 1899 and 1902, respectively.

The Germans, seeking a way to break the stalemate on the Western Front, were the first to discard this convention. The great chemist Fritz Haber, working with Walther Nernst, professor of chemistry at the University of Berlin, prepared materials for a weaponized chlorine gas, and also developed a gas mask. In 1916 Haber was made chief of the chemical warfare section, and in 1917 his department introduced mustard gas and experimented with other substances.

The first poison-gas attack was launched at Ypres on April 22nd, 1915. The British had

shock, but where it was not backed up by reserves; and at Caporetto in Italy in 1917, where a carefully coordinated assault that used chemical weapons alongside every other stratagem available resulted in the most crushing defeat of any of the Western European Allies in the First World War. The relatively small numbers of gas casualties reflected the limited investment in chemical warfare, with chemical shells accounting for only 4.5 percent of all shells and specialized chemical forces accounting for only 2 percent of the total engineer strength.

Gas was one of the most feared weapons, but its reputation was not backed up by the figures, for gas was less lethal than other weapons, particularly once decent gas masks had been developed and troops were trained in how to respond to a gas attack. Even the Americans, who were relatively poorly trained in gas drills and hence suffered over a quarter of their 258,000 casualties due to gas, suffered only a 2 percent mortality rate among these casualties versus a 25 percent mortality rate for other weapons.

The Second World War saw the major combatants stockpiling masses of chemical agents and, in the case of Germany, researching new and more deadly nerve agents such as sarin. But only the Japanese actually used chemical weapons in combat, in limited amounts in China. After the Second World War, research and stockpiling continued. The US was falsely accused of using chemical agents in Korea, but its use of herbicides, such as Agent Orange, in Vietnam and Cambodia, did arouse

huge controversy. The only substantiated instances of chemical weapons use since then have come from Iraq, where Saddam Hussein's forces used chemical weapons against the Iranians, and later against their own people at Halabja in 1988; Japan, where the Aum Shinrikyo cult used sarin in a series of terror attacks in 1994–5; and most recently in Syria, where state forces are generally accepted to have used chemical weapons against rebels. Working to prevent the use of such weapons and to encourage disarmament is the Organization for the Prohibition of Chemical Weapons, which was awarded the Nobel Peace Prize in 2013 in recognition of its efforts.

By 1917, when these Australian troops posed with their respirators, gas masks had become highly effective at reducing the impact of poison-gas attacks.

32

Inventor(s):
Ernest Swinton, W.G. Wilson, and others

Mk I/IV
TANK

Type:

Armored vehicle

Social

Political

Tactical ◼

Technical ◼

1915

A tank is an armored vehicle running on tracks, which allow it to cross almost any terrain that an infantry soldier can cover. Modern tanks can all trace their lineage back to a strange machine that lumbered around a factory yard in Lincoln, England, in late 1915.

Ernest Swinton

Modern siege engines

Many of the component ideas behind the tank — an armored gun platform capable of off-road maneuvers — had existed for a considerable period before 1915. In 1485 Leonardo da Vinci had proposed to the Duke of Milan an armored war machine with a conical, umbrellalike shield sat atop a circular base bristling with cannons pointed in all directions, which would be moved by wheels operated by hand cranks in the center of the platform. In 1898 F. R. Simms had mounted a Maxim machine gun on a motorbike to create a mobile gun platform. Jointed tracks — the key ingredient that would allow the tank to negotiate broken ground — had been invented in 1801 by Thomas German. And as early as 1904, turreted armored cars had been made for the Russians by the French firm Charron, Girardot et Voigt.

These components came together in the mind of British Lieutenant-Colonel Ernest Swinton in September 1914. Sent to France as an observer, he quickly grasped that the conflict had descended into siege warfare, and accordingly that what was needed were modern siege engines. In October Swinton saw some

Holt half-tracked "caterpillar" tractor, one of the inspirations for the tank.

American Holt caterpillar tractors moving artillery behind the lines, and he was struck with the notion of putting armor and guns on the tractor, as a way to answer the questions posed by the machine gun. As a result of discussions with Swinton, Maurice Hankey of the Committee of Imperial Defence wrote a paper in December proposing a machine with "caterpillar driving gear … [able to] run down barbed wire by sheer weight, to give some cover to men creeping up behind, and to support the advance with machine gun fire."

MK I/IV TANK

"Nobody wants them"

Swinton's proposal received the enthusiastic backing of Winston Churchill, then First Lord of the Admiralty, but in February 1915 the War Office dismissed the idea. Lord Kitchener argued: "the armored caterpillar would be shot up by guns." But Churchill, inspired by H. G. Wells' 1903 short story, "The Land Ironclads," pursued the project, reviving the proposal under Navy auspices, despite the opposition of the Fourth Sea Lord, who ranted that "Caterpillar landships are idiotic and useless. Nobody has asked for them and nobody wants them."

The first prototype, nicknamed "Little Willie," weighed 34.7 tons (31 tonnes) and carried two 6-pounder naval cannons and four machine guns; powered by 105 hp Daimler engines, it had a top speed of just 3.7 mph (5.9 kph). Built by Foster's of Lincoln, Little Willie consisted of a caterpillar chassis bearing an armored box, given the name "tank" by Swinton to help keep the project under wraps.

Little Willie proved problematic in field trials, because it kept "throwing" its tracks (i.e., the armor plate loop kept coming off the rollers), but the next prototype was already in development: Big Willie, also known as

"We heard strange throbbing noises, and lumbering slowly towards us came three huge mechanical monsters such as we had never seen before."

BERT CHANEY, SIGNAL OFFICER AT THE BATTLE OF THE SOMME, SEPTEMBER 1916

Little Willie undergoes field trials. Note the "rudder" steering assemblage at the rear.

"Wilson" (after its designer Major W. G. Wilson), "Mother" or "the Centipede," which would become the Mark I tank. It was rhomboidal in shape, with the track running all the way around the hull. The angled thrust of its hull helped it negotiate obstacles and the design meant it was much less likely to throw its tracks. In January to February 1916, Big Willie impressed observers, including King George V, and the War Office commissioned 100 units, later increased to 150, to be designated "His Majesty's Landship, Tank Mk I."

A "male"/destroyer Mk I tank in 1916 with grenade shield and steering rudder.

The experimental first deployment of the Mk I came in the third phase of the Battle of the Somme, in September 1916. An eyewitness, 19-year-old signal officer Bert Chaney, described their extraordinary appearance:

> [L]umbering slowly towards us came three huge mechanical monsters … Big metal things they were, with two sets of caterpillar wheels that went right round the body. There was a huge bulge on each side with a door in the bulging part, and machine guns on swivels poked out from either side.

The initial deployment did not go well. Most of the tanks ditched in unbridgeable shell holes or suffered engine failure, but those that made it to German lines had a huge impact, Chaney reported, "frightening the Jerries out of their wits and making them scuttle like frightened rabbits." One tank made it all the way to the village of Flers, "flattening everything they thought should be flattened, pushing down walls and thoroughly enjoying themselves … chasing and rounding up the Jerries, collecting thousands of prisoners and sending them back to our lines." A press report of this incident related: "A tank is walking up the High Street with the British Army cheering behind it."

These mechanical monsters were appalling to crew; the open engines spewed heat and toxic fumes into the cramped interior, where the crew risked severe injury from being thrown about and could communicate only through hand signals and taps. Yet the crews were sometimes forced to work 40-hour shifts. Something of the nature of the men who had to operate in these hellish circumstances is given by Chaney's account:

> The four men in the tank that had got itself hung up dismounted, all in the heat of the battle, stretching themselves, scratching their heads, then slowly and deliberately walked round their vehicle inspecting it from every angle and appeared to hold a conference among themselves. After standing around for a few minutes, looking somewhat lost, they calmly took out from the inside of the tank a primus stove and, using the side of the tank as a cover from enemy fire, sat down on the ground and made themselves some tea.

MK I/IV TANK

135

"It was magnificent"

Although the first deployment had been largely inauspicious due to the unsuitable terrain, partly attributable to the preliminary bombardment, British Commander-in-Chief Haig was sufficiently impressed to order rapid construction of a thousand more tanks, which would be the successor model to the Mk I, the Mk IV (Mks II and III perished in development). The Mk IV would have slightly improved steering, propulsion, and weapons. Like the Mk I, it would be constructed in two primary types: "male" ("destroyers" armed with cannon) and "female" ("man killers" armed only with machine guns, to help provide cover for the males).

The first serious deployment of tanks in battle came at Cambrai on November 20th, 1917. Around 380 fighting tanks went into battle carrying 1,000 guns, some with bundles of brushwood to create trench bridges. Discarding the usual preliminary bombardment resulted in total surprise and the attack was highly successful, penetrating 4 miles (6.4 km) past the front line and overrunning all the main trench systems. Captain D. G. Browne of "F" Batallion described the action: " ... had a grandstand view of ... "B" Battalion tanks ... racing down the Welsh Ridge ... It was magnificent and it was war all right ... The whole fleet took the wire in their stride ..." But the attack ran out of steam, with 179 tanks out of action and the crews of the rest exhausted; insufficient commitment of reserves enabled the Germans to scramble a new defensive line into place.

The Allied high command failed to appreciate the success of the tanks and they were not employed in this successful configuration again in the war, whereas the Germans were even slower to understand the potential of the device and did not start building tanks in earnest until 1918. By the end of the war only 45 German tanks had seen action, whereas the British had built 3,000.

Although the tank did not win the war, it did help strike a decisive blow when the British Fourth Army, armed with 450 tanks (mostly Mark Vs, along with some French tanks), broke through at Amiens on August 8th, 1918, and killed or captured 28,000 men and 400 guns. General Erich Ludendorff declared it "in the history of the war, the German army's Black Day."

British tanks parade through London to mark the end of the First World War.

The Mk I/IV Tank

[A] Rhomboidal shape
[B] Sponson (gun turret)
[C] Six-pounder cannon
[D] Driver's cab
[E] Caterpillar tracks

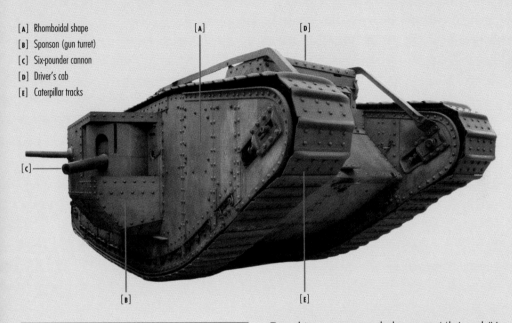

KEY FEATURE:
CATERPILLAR TRACKS

The tracks gave the vehicle the ability to go where wheeled vehicles feared to drive. The rhomboidal design of the Mk I, with the tracks running around the outside of the hull, meant that it had an equivalent "wheelspan" to a wheeled vehicle with 60-foot (18 m) wide wheels! In the Mk II, one track plate in six was wider to give better support on soft ground, and in the Mk IV every third, fifth, or ninth plate had a steel stud for better traction.

Two drivers were needed to steer Mk I and IV tanks. They sat at the front of the tank, in front of the engine, with a visor flap in front for viewing, and an overhead hatch for exit/escape. Only in later models was the engine isolated from the crew, who were exposed to the horrendous noise, fumes, and heat. The power generated by the engine was passed through a gearbox to epicyclic gears mounted on the sides of the hull, and these sent power through chain drives to reduction gears that engaged directly with the drive sprockets, the teeth of which engaged the track. Behind the engine were the storage racks for the 6-pound shells.

MK I/IV TANK

33

Inventor(s):
John T. Thompson

THOMPSON SUBMACHINE GUN

Type:

Submachine gun

Social ■

Political

Tactical ■

Technical

1918

One of the most iconic firearms in history, the Thompson heralded the advent of an entirely new class of gun: the submachine gun (originally known as the machine pistol by the Germans and the machine carbine by the British). Though not the first nor the best, it was undoubtedly the essential submachine gun, becoming a much-loved weapon in both peacetime and war.

John Thompson with his iconic gun.

The trench broom

The first submachine gun (SMG) is often said to have been the Italian Villar-Perosa of 1914 (introduced by the Italian Army in 1915), but this was really a light machine gun. In 1918 designers on both sides of the Atlantic, responding to the demands of trench warfare, independently originated true submachine guns. In Germany Hugo Schmeisser designed the Bergmann MP18/1, and in America General John Taliaferro Thompson invented his eponymous gun, inspired by the need for what he described as "a one-man, handheld machine gun. A trench broom!" The ordinary soldier, he recognized, rarely needed long-range precision; in trench warfare he was far more likely to need to deliver high-volume, short-range fire — something that would let him, in Thompson's words, "wipe out a whole company single-handed."

Thompson had been Chief of Small Arms for the US Ordnance Department and Chief Design Engineer for the Remington Arms Corporation, where he had helped to develop the Springfield M1903 rifle and the Colt M1911 pistol before setting up his own company,

Auto-Ordnance. When America joined the war, Thompson set about developing his "trench broom." Purchasing the patent for the delayed blowback mechanism invented by Navy Commander John N. Blish, he devised a delayed-blowback, air-cooled automatic weapon that took the same ammunition as the Colt pistol: .45 ACP. The ammunition was fed in from a 50-round drum magazine; in later models a 20 to 30-round box magazine was used.

Police and thieves

The first shipment of Thompson prototypes arrived on the dock in New York, ready to be shipped to Europe, on November 11th, 1918, the day that the Armistice was signed. Auto-Ordnance was left with a large inventory of guns, and little enthusiasm among the military. The weapon was marketed heavily at law-enforcement agencies, but sales were still low. Thompson lost control of the company, and Auto-Ordnance started to hawk the submachine guns through every legal outlet available. It was possible to purchase one by mail order or from

THOMPSON SUBMACHINE GUN

a local hardware or sporting goods store. But the price tag was too steep for middle-income America: the M1921 Thompson cost between $200 and $245, equivalent to two months' wages for a middle-class earner.

As it happens, however, this period saw the unexpected arrival of a new class of high-income gun enthusiasts. The advent of Prohibition in 1920 inadvertently triggered an explosion in the black economy as vast wealth poured into the hands of bootleggers, smugglers, and gangsters. The Thompson gun quickly became a firm favorite, notoriously being used in the St. Valentine's Day Massacre in 1929.

"Chicago gangland leaders observed Valentine's Day with machine guns and a stream of bullets and as a result seven members of the George (Bugs) Moran–Dean O'Banion, North Side Gang are dead in the most cold-blooded gang massacre in the history of this city's underworld," reported *The New York Times* the following day. "One of the men in police uniform probably gave the order to line up, face to the wall … Then, it is believed, came the order to 'give it to them' and the roar of the shotguns mingled with the rat-a-tat of the machine gun, a clatter like that of a gigantic type-writer." The tommy gun, also known as the Chicago typewriter, was also the weapon of choice for Depression-era bandits such as Bonnie and Clyde, John Dillinger, and "Pretty Boy" Floyd.

The tommy gun's involvement in the St. Valentine's Day Massacre indirectly led to the establishment of the most influential early American forensic lab, the Scientific Crime Detection Laboratory, when Calvin Goddard, a pioneering forensic scientist and gun enthusiast, was able to show by microscopic forensic firearm examination that all the men had been murdered by just two tommy guns. The massacre and similar outrages would also galvanize public opinion, culminating eventually in the 1934 National Firearms Act — the Thompson submachine gun can thus claim to be the weapon that led to the first national gun-control legislation in the US.

Belatedly, law enforcement agencies began to equip themselves with tommy guns. "Sold only on the side of Law and Order," proclaimed the marketing material produced by Auto-Ordnance, somewhat wishfully, insisting, "That's why bandits surrender to the man with the Thompson Gun — they know 'There's no getaway against a Thompson!'"

In the army now

The US military eventually started to adopt the Thompson SMG, starting with the coast guard, followed by the navy in 1928 and the marines in the 1930s, with the army eventually signing up in 1938. But it was the Germans and the Soviets who had been making the running in the field of submachine guns. In the late 1920s, Germany and the USSR had entered into a secret co-operation on weapons development, with the Soviets hoping to take advantage of German technical expertise and the Germans looking to circumvent the restrictions imposed by the Versailles Treaty of 1919. The end results were the German MP 38 and the Soviet Degtyarev

The Birger Gang poses for a group portrait at its hangout, Shady Rest, in Illinois, 1926. Leader Charley Birger is seated atop the driver's door, with a bulletproof vest and Thompson submachine gun.

PPD. The Soviets would go on to mass-produce SMGs, such as the PPSh 41, which they saw as the perfect weapon for often poorly trained soldiers to use in the close-quarters combat tactics favored by the Russian commanders. But it was the Germans who were initially best equipped with and made best use of the SMG. The MP 38 played an important role in Blitzkrieg tactics; after 1940 it was replaced by a cheaper version, the MP 40. Both were mistakenly nicknamed the Schmeisser, after the German gun designer behind an entirely different firearm. Over a million MP 40s were produced.

Also mass-produced was the British Sten (named for the initials of its inventors Shepherd

"Any man in your force who can shoot a pistol can shoot a Thompson better!"

Auto-Ordnance 1927 Thompson price list

and Turpin and the small arms factory at Enfield), which cost a twentieth as much as the Thompson: the Mark I, issued in 1941, cost about £2.50 to make. Although it was unreliable and liable to accidental discharge — and therefore unpopular with many — nearly 4 million had been produced by 1945, many of them supplied to resistance groups.

Meanwhile, the Thompson had been modified and simplified for military service. The M1A1 version had no foregrip and no drum magazine, with a simpler blowback mechanism. It was popular with troops from the Pacific to Europe. The Thompson continued to be produced after the war (some 1.7 million Thompson submachine guns have been made since 1921), but SMGs came to be largely superseded by assault rifles. Modern SMGs, like the Uzi and the Ingram, tend to be closer to machine pistols than guns.

THOMPSON SUBMACHINE GUN

34

Inventor(s):

John M. Browning

BROWNING M2
HEAVY MACHINE GUN

Type:

Heavy machine gun

Social

Political

Tactical

Technical

"The mounted lance of the US cavalry."

DEFENSE INDUSTRY DAILY

1921

The M2 heavy machine gun, affectionately nicknamed the Ma Deuce, is one of the most versatile, long-lived, and effective weapons in the history of firearms. Amazingly, it remains a crucial and ubiquitous element of the arsenal of the modern military, nearly a century after its original incarnation first appeared, and with minimal differences from the versions used since the start of the Second World War.

John M. Browning

Unstoppable

Heavy machine guns have become the crucial enabling tool in the philosophy of battlefield dominance through superior firepower, and the Browning M2 is the dominant weapon in this field. It started life as a lighter machine gun, all the way back in 1900, when John M. Browning received his first patent for a recoil-operated machine gun. By 1910 he had produced a 0.3-caliber, tripod-mounted machine gun with a water-cooling jacket that could fire at up to 500 rpm. His design had major advantages over the Maxim (see page 112), which had cornered the lucrative European market: it was shorter and lighter, weighing around 93 pounds (42 kg) with all its accessories, compared to around 140 pounds (64 kg) for a Maxim; and its recoil sliding-block locking mechanism was much simpler than the Maxim's, making it cheaper and easier to manufacture and maintain. However, there was limited interest in Browning's design in America until the entry of the US into the First World War in 1917. Belatedly realizing that they had almost no machine guns, the US military called for domestic candidates; Browning, who had

quietly perfected his 1910 design, came forward to give a demonstration at the Government Proving Ground at Springfield Armory, in May 1917. The test involved the candidate weapon firing 20,000 rounds; Browning's gun fired all 20,000 without a single hitch or broken part. To the amazement of the observers, he then fired off another 20,000 rounds with one minor component failure, getting through 40 cases of ammunition in just over two hours.

The M1917 went into mass production but arrived too late to affect the course of the First World War. But it was so effective that it continued to give impressive service throughout and beyond the Second World War. In one legendary action, Marine platoon sergeant Mitchell Paige found himself in charge of an M1917 machine gun section that was the only thing preventing a Japanese breakthrough in the Solomon Islands. "I continued to trigger bursts until the barrel began to steam," he later recalled. "In front of me was a large pile of dead bodies. I ran around the ridge from gun to gun trying to keep them firing, but at each

A tripod-mounted M2HB assists in the liberation of a French town in Normandy, in the summer of 1944.

emplacement, I found only dead bodies. I knew then I must be all alone." At Guadalcanal Marine Gunnery Sergeant John Basilone famously used his M1917 machine gun to "virtually annihilate a Japanese regiment," according to the official report. Basilone was killed on Iwo Jima but is memorialized in a statue that shows him carrying an M1917.

Bigger and harder

Toward the end of the First World War the American commander-in-chief John Pershing put out a call for a heavier machine gun with armor-piercing capabilities and a long enough range to be used for antiaircraft, tank, and artillery fire. Browning adapted the M1917 into the M1921, which fired massive .50-inch caliber bullets. After Browning's death the gun was further developed in the 1930s to become the M2 heavy machine gun, used in slightly different incarnations in a multitude of roles, from infantry support to being mounted on

ships, aircraft, tanks, and jeeps, and even as antiaircraft emplacements. In aircraft the M2 could be air-cooled, and on ships where weight was less of a problem it could be water-cooled, but for land-based applications the water jacket was dropped to save weight. However, this led to rapid overheating of the barrel, and to counteract this a heavier, thicker barrel was introduced that would absorb and dissipate heat. The result was the definitive M2HB (for heavy barrel), introduced in 1933 and still going strong today.

The combination of heavy-caliber bullet and high muzzle velocity of 2,920 feet per second (890 m/s) gave the M2 massive power over very long ranges: its maximum effective range for aimed fire is 2,000 yards (1,829 m), but its bullets can reach up to 7,440 yards (6,803 m). The .50-caliber armor-piercing rounds could easily penetrate engine blocks, hull plates, and fuel tanks of enemy aircraft, half-tracks, and light armored cars. The M2 was also reliable; by the end of the Second World War operators could expect one jam for every 4,000 rounds fired. Between 1941 and 1945 US arms factories made nearly 2 million M2 guns, of which over 400,000 were M2HBs for ground use. Since the Browning .50 caliber was first invented, in 1921, some 3 million have been manufactured.

The Meat Chopper

The M2HB achieved particular success in Europe after D-Day. German aviators are known to have particularly hated the gun, which, when mounted on tanks and other vehicles, provided lethal antiaircraft protection for convoys that would otherwise have been sitting ducks. One of the most feared configurations was the "Meat Chopper," a quad .50 caliber set-up mounted on wheels. Ostensibly an antiaircraft weapon, it proved useful against German snipers hidden in trees: the quad gunner would simply blast the trunk into splinters, collapsing the tree and taking the sniper with it.

Since the First World War the M2 has been used in almost every conflict and is a primary weapon for the militaries of over 75 nations. It has even been used as a sniper weapon. Legendary Marine sniper Carlos Hatchcock fitted an M2HB with a telescopic sight and used it to kill a Viet Cong soldier at a range of nearly 2,460 yards (2,250 m); until 1992 the longest confirmed sniper kill ever. M2HBs have featured in heroic actions such as the one that won Audie Murphy, the most decorated American soldier of the Second World War, his Congressional Medal of Honor in France in January 1945. Murphy leaped on top of a burning tank destroyer and used his M2HB to kill dozens of Germans and fight off a tank unit, withstanding intense enemy fire for an hour and eventually forcing the German tanks to withdraw.

An M45 Quadmount .50 caliber antiaircraft set-up, also known as the Meat Chopper, complete with "tombstone" ammunition can for each gun.

35

Inventor(s):
John C. Garand

M1 GARAND

Type:

Semiautomatic rifle

Social

Political

Tactical ■

Technical ■

> "In my opinion, the M1 rifle is the greatest battle implement ever devised."
>
> GENERAL GEORGE S. PATTON, JR.

1936

The M1 Garand was the first semiautomatic rifle to be issued as standard to a nation's infantry when it was adopted by the US Army in 1936. As a result, the US military went into the Second World War equipped with a better infantry rifle than any of the other participants — a rifle that excited admiration and envy from other fighting forces and affection from the men equipped with it. General Patton famously called it "the greatest battle implement ever devised," whereas General Douglas McArthur opined: "this Garand rifle is one of the greatest contributions to our armed forces."

Mechanical questions

Ever since Maxim invented the first successful automatic weapon (see page 112), small arms designers had set their sights on extending the principles of automated reloading to smaller weapons. But these self-same principles are inherently problematic for small arms — the basis of automated reloading is to use the forces generated by the explosion of the powder charge, in one way or another, to drive the automatic mechanism. Maxim, for instance, used the force of recoil, whereas Browning's seminal heavy machine gun used the force of the exhaust or muzzle gases generated by the combustion of the powder charge. But these forces can be extremely powerful, requiring strong, heavy mechanisms that can cope with intense pressure, heat, and impact. Such mechanisms are fine in a machine gun, a heavy weapon expected to be supported on a tripod or fixed on a mount, but their weight makes them impractical for use in a shoulder rifle of the sort that forms the workhorse of infantry armaments. The smaller, less powerful ammunition used in pistols generates less intense forces, and so automatic (or

semiautomatic) pistols appeared very quickly and were successful. But a successful shoulder rifle employing automatic principles was a much harder nut to crack.

The obstacles to developing such a weapon were recognized early on. In 1902, shortly after the adoption of the M1903 Springfield bolt-action rifle as the standard-issue weapon of the US military, the Chief of Ordnance described the challenge:

> Both tactical and mechanical questions are involved in the consideration of the possible desirability of the substitution of a semiautomatic musket for the hand-operated magazine rifle. Up to the present time mechanical invention has not solved its part of the problem, and no rifle of the class has been presented to this Department for examination and test …

Nonetheless, the US military remained interested in developing a successor to the M1903 Springfield that would be semiautomatic. "Semi-" indicates that expulsion of the empty cartridge and chambering of the next round are automatic, but

M1 GARAND

that each shot requires a separate pull of the trigger — to the top brass this made more sense than a fully automatic weapon, which would see the common soldier wastefully expend all his ammunition at once. Whereas a manually reloaded rifle such as a bolt-action Springfield required the soldier to break his line of sight and re-aim for each shot, a semiautomatic would allow him to observe the accuracy of his first shot and instantly make the adjustments necessary for his next shots, as well as dramatically increasing the rate of fire achievable.

Almost as soon as the First World War was over, the US Ordnance Board began to pursue the semiautomatic rifle. There had been a number of successful semiautomatic hunting rifles by this time, but these used relatively low-power ammunition. The main obstacle facing the Ordnance Board was that the main service cartridge of the US military was the .30-06 caliber, which, according to Major General Julian Hatcher, who was personally involved in the development of the semiautomatic rifle and went on to write *Hatcher's Book of the Garand*, was:

> ... one of the most powerful cartridges used by any shoulder rifle ... It had a 150-grain bullet driven at a muzzle velocity of 2,700 feet per second [823 m/s] by a charge of smokeless powder giving a maximum pressure of 50,000 pounds per square inch, while the average 'high power' cartridge of those days, of either the military or the hunting type, had a normal chamber pressure of around 40,000 pounds [18,144 kg] per square inch, and a muzzle velocity of around 2,100 feet per second [640 m/s], more or less.

This high-powered bullet placed too great a strain on the rifle actions available; according to Hatcher, they:

> ... simply were not anywhere nearly strong enough ... Moreover, the heat generated by sustained fire with the high-pressure cartridge and its large powder charge was so severe that extraction became very difficult after only a few shots, and the stocks and hand guards were badly charred after a burst of a hundred shots rapid fire.

The most successful solution came from the work of a Canadian-born weapons designer, John Cantius Garand. In 1919, recognizing the promise of his early designs, the Springfield Armory (the main ordnance developer for the US military) took him on as an engineer. Developing a gas-operated design, in which the muzzle gases generated by the charge detonation were tapped to drive a piston, which would turn a rotating breech mechanism, Garand spent the 1920s refining a .276-caliber prototype. In 1932 this was deemed successful enough to be on the verge of being commissioned, but General MacArthur, then Secretary of War and Army Chief of Staff, stepped in and insisted that .276 cartridges were underpowered, and that the version of the rifle intended for the .30-06 cartridges be developed instead. Fortunately, Garand had pursued this model as well, and in 1933 his design was designated the Semiautomatic Rifle, Caliber 30, M1. By 1936 it was ready to be adopted into service, although refinements to and simplification of the gas mechanism meant that it did not achieve its final, successful form until 1941.

John Garand points out the salient features of his rifle to senior US generals, 1944.

Love at first sight

The resulting weapon was powerful, rugged, and reliable. It proved enormously popular with servicemen. Gilbert Lewis, a soldier who went through basic training in the 1950s, recalled:

> When I was issued my Garand, I knew it was love at first sight … I immediately took to its wonderful lines, almost feminine in its outward appearance … I was so smitten with the M1 that I even cleaned my barrack buddies!

Robert Wilson recalled the day he qualified with his rifle in basic training:

> I was never more proud to be an American soldier and know that my M1 Garand rifle was a weapon without equal and a rifle that I could trust in any situation.

A 2008 article in NRA's *American Rifleman* magazine rated the M1 Garand the number one infantry rifle of all time.

The weapon did have one drawback, though. The Garand was loaded with a clip of eight bullets that were pushed into the receiver.

When they were all used, the clip would be ejected with a loud "ping," regarded as one of the foremost drawbacks of the weapon as it gave away the position of the firer and helpfully informed his enemy when he was out of bullets.

Over the course of the Second World War the Springfield and Winchester armories turned out 4 million M1 rifles, making the Garand the most widely used semiautomatic rifle of the war. The M1 continued as the standard US infantry weapon through the Korean War: almost one and a half million new M1s were produced between 1952 and 1957, and eventually around 6 million M1 Garand rifles were made. As a government employee, however, the eponymous weapons designer received not a cent of royalties. There was an attempt to pass a Congressional resolution to reward Garand with a special bonus of $100,000, but it was not passed.

36

Mikhail Koshkin and the Kharkov Locomotive Factory

T-34 TANK

Social ■

Political

Tactical ■

Technical

Type:

Armored vehicle

1939–40

The identity of the "best tank of the Second World War" is the subject of fierce debate, with the T-34, a Soviet medium tank, being a popular candidate. Even if the claims of the German Panzer Mk V or other contenders are preferred, it is hard to deny that the T-34 was the most important tank of the war — probably the most important tank ever, and arguably the most important weapon of the Second World War.

Tank warfare

The tutorial offered by the First World War on the importance of tanks to modern warfare was quickly forgotten by Britain, the US, and France, as they downgraded or discarded their tank forces. In the US, for instance, the Tank Corps was abolished altogether in 1920. But the Russians and Germans recognized the value of mobile armor. In 1932 the Russians raised mechanized corps of a hundred tanks each — seven of them by 1938. Meanwhile, the Germans developed a series of Panzer models and raised six Panzer divisions. They also attended keenly to the new gospel of tank warfare being preached by British theorists J. F. C. Fuller and Basil Liddell Hart. Prophets without honor in their own land, their work became the basis for the doctrine of *Blitzkrieg* (lightning war), which used massive concentrations of armor as the spearheads for powerful breakthroughs that would be comprehensively followed up and resourced so that the tanks could advance rapidly and relentlessly. The power and mobility offered by tanks would be realized in devastating fashion by the Germans in 1940 as they swept through Europe. The scanty and scattered Allied armor was able to put up little resistance to the Panzer Divisions and it took the Germans just 60 days to conquer Western Europe.

The perfect balance

The only serious threat to the might of German armor at this point was the mass of tanks built up by the Soviets. By 1941 the Germans had built around 5,000 tanks; the Soviets had constructed 21,000 to 24,000 tanks and were churning them out at four times the rate that German factories could manage. According to Hasso von Manteuffel, commander of the German 7th Panzer Division, "Fire-power, armor protection, speed, and cross-country performance are the essentials, and the best type of tank is that which combines these conflicting requirements with the most success." The best of the Russian tanks was the T-34, which, of all the contemporary tanks, combined "these conflicting requirements" most effectively. "Their T-34 was the best in the world," wrote German tank general, Field Marshal Paul Ludwig Ewald von Kleist.

T-34 TANK

Red Army soldiers and Soviet T-34 tanks on the attack during the Battle of Kursk, July 1943.

The genesis of the T-34 lay with the 1931 purchase by the Russians of two American Christie tanks, the advanced suspension system of which would become the basis for that of the T-34. To power the tank, Soviet engineers worked, ironically, from a German model: a BMW diesel engine. Built from lightweight aluminum, the engine developed for the T-34 became the first practical diesel engine for a tank. It offered improved range and reliability and 30 percent more power than any other contemporary tank engine, and it was robust, with a low risk of catching fire if damaged.

The T-34 armor was 1.77 inches (45 mm) thick, when most German tanks had 1.18 inches (30 mm), and it had sloping sides and rounded edges to help deflect shells. Meanwhile, the tank's own gun — initially a 3-inch (76 mm) — had enough power to pierce the armor of most other tanks. The tank's high power–weight ratio and wide tracks, combined with the Christie suspension, gave it superb off-road mobility, with the ability to run across snow and mud, and it had a high speed of 32 mph (51 kph) versus around 22 mph (35 kph) for a Panzer III/IV. Perhaps most importantly, the simple, rugged design of the T-34 made it easy to manufacture in high volumes and easy to repair.

"It was the most excellent example of the offensive weapon of the Second World War."

FRIEDRICH WILHELM VON MELLENTHIN

The tank's detractors counter many of the claims made for the superiority of the T-34. For instance, it was very cramped, with no consideration for crew comfort or safety. Only 25 to 30 percent of crews survived the destruction of their vehicles — in 1943 alone, 14,000 T-34 tank crewmen were lost. It could also be heard from 547 yards (0.5 km) away, so that the enemy often had time to prepare countermeasures.

Weight of numbers

Developed under Mikhail Koshkin at the Kharkov Tractor Factory in the Ukraine, the first prototype of the T-34 was completed in early 1939. Koshkin proved its range and robustness by leading the first two prototypes on an arduous round trip of 1,790 miles (2,880 km), in bitter weather in early 1940, a journey that cost him his life when he contracted pneumonia. The tank was promptly accepted into service and went into production in mid-1940 as the T-34/76 (referring to the caliber of the gun). It would eventually be made at six different factories, with more T-34s being constructed than any other tank in the Second World War. By the time of the German invasion on June 22nd, 1941, some 1,225 of the tanks had been built; the threat posed by this growing force of Soviet tanks may have been a significant factor behind Hitler's decision to launch the invasion.

Initially, German armor overmatched Soviet forces and the Germans advanced across vast swathes of the USSR. But by 1943 the balance of the war had shifted decisively against Germany, thanks not to strategy or battlefield defeats, but to simple weight of economic and industrial numbers, primarily the production of tanks. In 1943 Germany produced 5,966 tanks, just double its 1941 output; in the same year the Americans produced 21,000 tanks, the British 8,000, and the Soviets over 15,000. It took just 3,000 man hours to build a T-34 versus 55,000 man hours to make a Panzer; although prices are hard to quantify for command economies on a war footing, the Russian tank cost roughly half as much as a Panzer to make: US$25,470 versus US$51,600 in 1943 dollar terms.

The ultimate clash between German and Soviet tanks came at the Battle of Kursk in July 1943, and it was here that the great disparity in scale of production would tell. The Germans massed 2,000 tanks, but found themselves facing nearly 6,000 Russian tanks, along with a further 6,000 anti-tank guns. The Russians weathered the German assault before counterattacking with their T-34s, eventually destroying nearly half of the German tank fleet.

German tank design improved markedly to meet the challenge of the T-34; the German Panzer V is widely considered to have been the best all-round tank of the Second World War, but it was too little, too late. By 1944 the T-34 had been equipped with a massive 85-mm gun that could destroy the new, heavily armored Panzer V and Tiger tanks, and in that year alone the Russians built 11,000 T-34/85s. By the end of the Second World War the Russians had built more than 80,000 T-34s. The T-34 continued to see service until well after the Second World War; in some countries, the tank was still in service more than 60 years later.

37

Inventor(s):

Fritz Gosslau, Walter Dornberger, Wernher von Braun, and others

V WEAPONS

Social ■

Political

Tactical

Technical ■

Type:

Flying bomb and ballistic rocket missile

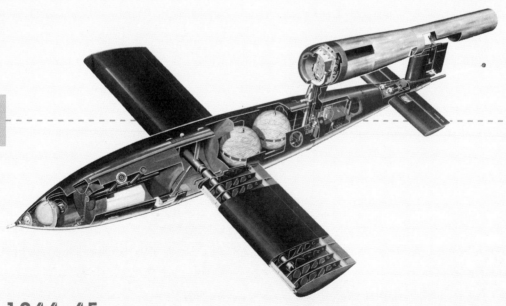

1944–45

The *Vergeltungswaffen*, or "Vengeance Weapons," of 1944–45 had limited tactical or strategic impact, but their psychological impact, and the death and destruction they visited on thousands of families, were immense. Also enormously significant was their importance for the future of weapons and many other fields of technology.

Rocket men

The two main V weapons were the V-1 flying bomb (essentially a pilotless jet plane, forerunner of modern cruise missiles), also known as the Fiesler Fi-103, and the V-2 rocket. Development of the V-2 started in the early 1930s. Under the terms of the Treaty of Versailles, which had brought the First World War to a close, Germany was forbidden to develop new artillery weapons, but the treaty

Illustration from an early 15th-century manuscript showing Alexander the Great brandishing a mysterious weapon, believed to be the first depiction of a rocket in Western literature.

said nothing about rockets. Traditionally viewed as a curiosity of little practical military value, rockets date back to early medieval China, and were probably the first gunpowder weapons ever made.

A rocket is a device driven by the Newtonian principle (from his third law of motion) that the action of a force produces an equal and opposite reaction: thus, hot gas blasting out from one end will drive a rocket forward in the direction of the other end. A rocket is essentially a tube, open at one end, filled with propellant — material that will blast out of the open end to propel the rocket forward. Propellant can be anything from water under pressure to compressed air to explosives that will generate hot gas. Because a rocket generates its own thrust, it does not produce recoil in the launcher, and hence can be launched from a relatively lightweight frame while still generating tremendous kinetic energy by the time of impact.

Chinese and Indian armies made some use of rockets, and experience with Indian rockets led Englishman Sir William Congreve to develop "Congreve" rockets. Used by British and American armies in the early 19th century, they could not match the power, range, or accuracy of artillery, and the science of rocketry languished in military circles, although farsighted science-fiction writers and enthusiasts recognized their potential, among them the German *Verein fur Raumschiffarht* (VfR, German Rocket Society).

When the German military conceived an interest in rockets, artillery officer Walter Dornberger was commissioned to develop the idea. He contacted the VfR and in 1932 recruited the services of an enthusiastic and brilliant young engineer, Wernher von Braun. Together they began developing liquid-fuel rockets for the military, but the process proved difficult. A small initial prototype known as the A2 had limited success in late 1934, but it took another decade to develop the large A4 rocket, with a range of 200 miles (322 km) and effective guidance and control systems. Powered by an engine that mixed alcohol with hydrogen

A German crew rolls a V-1 to the launch site.

peroxide, it could accelerate beyond the speed of sound within 30 seconds, blasting 60 miles (97 km) up into the atmosphere. But the expense and complexities of the rocket program, together with its slow pace of development, meant that it found little favor with the Nazi hierarchy until the success of the V-1 weapon caught their attention.

Buzz bombs

The V-1 flying bomb was primarily the brainchild of Fritz Gosslau, an employee of Argus Motoren aircraft engine manufacturers, a company that had produced a remote-controlled surveillance plane. Gosslau refined an ingenious and simple yet sophisticated pulse jet engine, which had few moving parts and hence was relatively reliable. In the pulse-jet, "pulses" of air were combined with doses of fuel and the mixture was ignited with a spark plug; the force of the combustion drove shut the front intake shutters and the exhaust gases were expelled from the rear of the engine, producing thrust. With the pressure relieved the front intake shutters reopened to admit another pulse of air and the process repeated. The engine cycled through around 50 pulses per second, producing a distinctive buzzing sound that Londoners came to dread, and which earned the weapon nicknames such as the buzz bomb and the doodlebug.

Flying bomb proposals were twice rejected by the Luftwaffe, in 1939 and again in 1941, but in 1942 the go-ahead was given to develop the project. Together with Robert Lusser of Fieseler, Gosslau designed a craft with a single pulse jet

American ambulance women look on as workers search for survivors amid the wreckage inflicted by a V-1 flying bomb in South London in 1944.

mounted on a pod, above a fuselage with stubby wings and an explosive payload in the nose. The guidance and control system used gyroscopes for stability, a magnetic compass and barometric altimeter for heading and altitude control, and a simple vane anemometer (i.e., a small windmill) that drove a counter to determine when the engine should shut off, sending the bomb plummeting to earth to detonate.

In 1942 the Allies learned of the development of the V-1 from their spies, and from 1943 Churchill ordered Operation Crossbow to disrupt its production and launch. Allied bombers attacked the rocket research center at Peenemunde on the Baltic Sea, with limited effect, but had more success bombing launch sites, destroying 73 of the 96 launch sites built for the V-1. Where the Germans had hoped to launch 5,000 V-1s a month, they eventually managed to launch only 10,500 against Britain over an 80-day period.

The British quickly learned that antiaircraft guns could provide an effective defense against the bombs. Whereas the first weeks of the V-1 blitz did tremendous damage to London, the redeployment of antiaircraft guns to coastal areas proved highly effective. In the last four weeks of the V-1 offensive, the kill rate of antiaircraft defenses versus the flying bombs went from 24 percent to 46 percent, to 67 percent, to 79 percent in the final week. Even when the bombs got through they had limited tactical or strategic value — they were wildly inaccurate, and could only aim at an 8-mile (13 km) radius target circle (centered, for London attacks, on Tower Bridge). V-1s that hit Southampton, for instance, had actually been aimed at Portsmouth, about 16 miles (26 km)

A V-2 on the launchpad during Operation Backfire, a British program to evaluate the technology using captured rockets and rocket scientists.

"This is the decisive weapon of the war."

<small>ADOLF HITLER ON THE V-2, AS RELATED BY ALBERT SPEER IN HIS BOOK *INSIDE THE THIRD REICH*</small>

away. Churchill lambasted the V-1 as "a weapon of such gross inaccuracy. The flying bomb is a weapon literally and essentially indiscriminate in its nature, purpose, and effect."

Allied advances on the Continent pushed V-1 launch sites out of range of London, but in late 1944 the V-2 rocket was finally ready for use; the first was launched on September 8th, 1944, with 3,172 more following over the next six months. Because the V-2 was supersonic it could not be tracked, intercepted, or even heard, so there was no warning of an imminent strike — the sonic boom of the approaching rocket arrived only after the explosion. The V-2 was much deadlier than the V-1, with a death rate per missile of 11.06 versus 2.7 for the V-1 (in South London). The rockets spread terror throughout London, and in fact the British government used its double agents to convince the Nazis that they were so afraid that they had moved their offices to Dulwich, in the south of the city, thus fooling the missile aimers into changing their targeting. Around 115,000 people were killed or wounded by V-2s before the Allies overran their launching sites.

Albert Speer, Armaments Minister under the Nazis, insisted that if the Nazi top brass had supported the project the V weapons could have been operational months before D-Day. General Eisenhower, head of the Allied invasion forces, later wrote, "It seems likely that if the German had succeeded in perfecting and using these new weapons earlier than he did, our invasion of Europe would have proved exceedingly difficult, perhaps impossible."

V-1 Flying Bomb

[A] Windmill for range control
[B] Magnetic compass
[C] Warhead
[D] Fuel tank
[E] Compressed air tanks
[F] Gyro controls
[G] Pulse jet
[H] Rudder

The V-1 flying bomb was equipped with two fuse switches — one on the nose and one on the belly — to trigger detonation of the warhead in the event of either a nose or belly landing. The leading edges of the stubby wings were equipped with balloon cable cutters in an attempt to neutralize barrage balloons (air-defense blimps). The distinctive, banded spherical tanks held compressed air, which was used both to pressurize the adjacent fuel tank and to power the gyroscope and flight control actuators (which operated the flaps and rudder) that comprised the aircraft's control system.

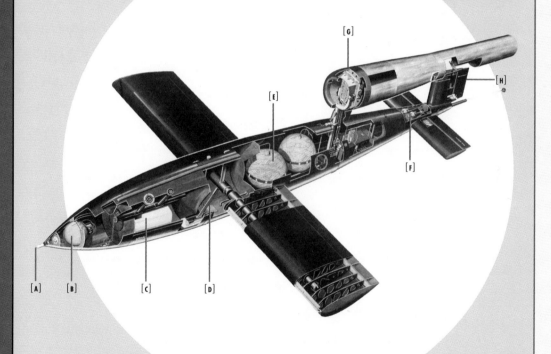

38

Inventor(s):
Manhattan Project

Mk1 "LITTLE BOY" ATOM BOMB

Type:

Nuclear weapon

Social

Political ■

Tactical ■

Technical ■

"I have been engaged in experiments which suggest that the atom can be artificially disintegrated. If this is true, it is of far greater importance than a war."

ERNEST RUTHERFORD, 1918

1945

"Little Boy" was the name given to the first atomic bomb, dropped on Hiroshima, Japan, on August 6th, 1945. Around 70,000 people were killed immediately, with a further 70,000 at least dying of injuries and radiation poisoning over the next few years. The bomb was the result of one of the greatest science and engineering projects of all time, and marked perhaps the most important military application of science in history. It radically changed the course of subsequent history, ushering in the nuclear age, the Cold War, and the continuing threat of global nuclear devastation.

Of great importance

The immense power latent in the atom had been recognized since the early years of the 20th century, most particularly in Einstein's famous formulation $e = mc^2$, which shows how a minuscule quantity of matter can be equivalent — if some means of conversion exists — to a colossal amount of energy; the equation explains that the energy content of a unit of matter is found by multiplication by the square of the speed of light in a vacuum, an astronomical quantity. Important early work on the structure of the atom was done by the physicist Ernest Rutherford. In 1918, serving on a committee for anti-submarine measures, he was told off for being late. "Speak softly, please," he responded. "I have been engaged in experiments which suggest that the atom can be artificially disintegrated. If this is true, it is of far greater importance than a war." As Bernard and Fawn Brodie point out in their history of weapons *From Crossbow to H-Bomb*, however, "His discoveries could not be more important than a war because they have made war so much more important."

The general consensus among scientists around this time was that the internal bonds that hold the nucleus of the atom together are so strong that there would be no way to alter them to release meaningful quantities of energy. Not all physicists agreed. In October 1933, Leo Szilard, one of the key figures in the development of the atom bomb, mused that "a chain reaction might be set up if an element could be found that would emit two neutrons when it swallows one neutron." A neutron is a subatomic particle that carries no charge; emission of neutrons from atomic nuclei is typically accompanied by the release of huge amounts of energy. Szilard recognized that if it were possible to generate a cascade of neutron emissions, an explosive amount of energy could be released.

Between 1930 and 1939, work by Enrico Fermi, Irène Joliot-Curie, Otto Hahn, Lise Meitner, Otto Frisch, and others confirmed the existence of the neutron and demonstrated that when an atom of uranium, the heaviest element then known, absorbs a neutron it becomes unstable and splits into two — a process that

MK1 "LITTLE BOY" ATOM BOMB

The atomic bomb "Little Boy" on its cradle shortly before being loaded onto the *Enola Gay* bomber.

Meitner and Frisch, in a 1939 paper in *Nature*, called "nuclear fission." They noted that fission releases a tremendous amount of energy, but it was Szilard who saw that the more important issue, from the point of view of weaponizing fission, is whether a chain reaction of neutron emissions can result from fission. In experiments at Columbia, where he had taken up residence having been driven out of Europe by the Nazis, Szilard found that it can. He was concerned enough about his discovery to begin warning fellow scientists that they ought to consider keeping their emerging research results under wraps.

The Uranium Project

Szilard, along with fellow émigré Jewish scientists Edward and Eugene Wigner, recruited Albert Einstein to write a letter to President Roosevelt, which the financier Alexander Sachs was enlisted to deliver in person. In October 1939, Sachs captured the president's attention with an apocryphal tale of how Napoleon had turned down the chance to develop a fleet of steamships that would have changed the course of history. Impressed with the potential of the nuclear project, Roosevelt famously called in his attaché, General "Pa" Wilson, declaring, "Pa, this requires action!" The US government's "Uranium Project" began work in July 1940.

Initial research focused on proving controlled chain reaction in a pile (a mass of mixed uranium isotopes); this was first achieved on December 2nd, 1942, in a pile constructed beneath the University of Chicago football stadium. For a bomb, however, uncontrolled chain reaction in a critical mass of one particular isotope of uranium (U-235) was desired, and U-235 accounts for just 6.7 percent of naturally occurring uranium. A November 1941 report of the National Academy Committee on the "Uranium Project" predicted that at least 4.4 pounds (2 kg) of U-235 would be required — this alone would require a huge engineering effort.

In June 1942 the research project, now under military auspices, was renamed the Manhattan District Project, and in 1942 Brigadier General Leslie R. Groves of the Corps of Engineers was put in charge. What resulted was a colossal scientific, engineering, and industrial program of unprecedented scale. A community of nuclear physicists under J. Robert Oppenheimer was created at Los Alamos in New Mexico to investigate the physics of the bomb itself. Of equal importance was the industrial-scale effort to separate uranium isotopes and produce enough U-235 for a bomb, which resulted in the construction of vast plants at Oak Ridge in Tennessee and Hanford in Washington.

Destroyer of worlds

On July 16th, 1945, the Manhattan Project's work came to fruition with the detonation of a test device in the New Mexico desert. The device exploded with a force of 22 kilotons (an explosion equivalent to 24,640 tons/22,000 tonnes of TNT). Oppenheimer said later that he "remembered the line from the Hindu scripture, the *Bhagavad Gita* … 'I am become death, the destroyer of worlds.'"

In addition to the test device, the Project had accumulated enough U-235 and plutonium to build two more bombs. The first, nicknamed "Little Boy," was a "gun"-type bomb. A pellet of U-235 of subcritical mass was fired into a receiver of U-235 also of subcritical mass; when combined they reached critical mass and set off an uncontrolled nuclear fission chain reaction. The bomb was loaded aboard the B-29 Superfortress *Enola Gay* and dropped over Hiroshima. It exploded 1,903 feet (580 m) above the ground, with a force of 15 kilotons, despite

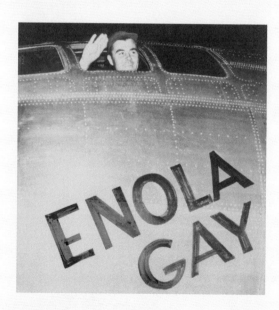

Paul Tibbets, pilot of the *Enola Gay*, named for his mother, waves from the cockpit before setting off to bomb Hiroshima.

"Fat Man," the bomb that was dropped on Nagasaki.

the bomb itself measuring just 10 feet by 28 inches (3 m x 71 cm), and containing just 140 pounds (64 kg) of uranium fuel. Directly beneath the explosion the temperature reached 3,870°C (6,998°F), and the flash set fire to clothes on people a mile and a quarter away. The shock wave at ground zero generated winds of 980 mph (1,577 kph) and pressure equivalent to 8,600 pounds per square foot (41,990 kg per square meter). Even a third of a mile away the wind speed was 620 mph (998 kph). Around 5 square miles (13 km²) of the city was flattened. The tail gunner of the *Enola Gay*, Staff Sergeant George Caron, described the view: "The mushroom cloud itself was a spectacular sight, a bubbling mass of purple-gray smoke and you

could see it had a red core in it and everything was burning inside … It looked like lava or molasses covering a whole city …" The co-pilot, Captain Robert Lewis, described how, "Where we had seen a clear city two minutes before, we could no longer see the city. We could see smoke and fires creeping up the sides of the mountains."

Three days later the plutonium bomb "Fat Man" was dropped on Nagasaki, and Japan duly surrendered. The atomic bomb had brought the Second World War to a close, but it had opened the door to a new age of global insecurity and nuclear terror.

"The force from which the Sun draws its power has been loosed against those who brought war to the Far East."

PRESIDENT HARRY TRUMAN, ON BEING INFORMED OF THE DESTRUCTION OF HIROSHIMA

The mushroom cloud rises over Nagasaki; beneath it, a 3-mile (4.8 km) area is enveloped by the blast, killing 40,000 people instantly and destroying a third of the city's buildings.

39

Inventor(s):
Mikhail Kalashnikov

KALASHNIKOV
AK-47

Type:

Assault rifle

Social ■

Political ■

Tactical

Technical

"There are scores of variants of Kalashnikov assault
rifles made in dozens of countries […] They all
owe their roots to Mikhail Kalashnikov."

GORDON ROTTMAN, *THE AK-47*, (2011)

1947

The AK-47 was the brainchild of Mikhail Kalashnikov. Direct combat experience during the Second World War, backed up with a pre-war interest in engineering, meant that Kalashnikov was well placed to develop a new infantry gun. Wounded in the Battle of Bryansk (1943), he began sketching the conceptual outline of what was to become the AK-47 — this archetypal assault weapon — while in the hospital.

Mikhail Kalashnikov

Propaganda and plagiarism

Kalashnikov had been informed that a new weapon was required for the 0.3 x 1.53-inch (7.62 x 39 mm) cartridge developed by Elisarov and Semin in 1943. His original concept did not win approval from the Soviet military authorities. Instead, the Sudayev PPS43 submachine gun was preferred. However, as a decorated war hero, Kalashnikov's involvement in the project had propaganda benefits for the Soviet Union, regardless of any other successful designs. So he went back to the drawing board as the leader of a team of designers and engineers. The resulting design incorporated elements derived from the German Sturmgewehr 44 (the gas-operated system and general layout), the Remington Model 8 rifle (the safety mechanism), and the M1 Garand rifle (the trigger and forestock). Yet it would be unfair to accuse Mikhail Kalashnikov of stealing design innovations from either the Germans or the Americans. The process of assault-weapon development was an evolutionary one, in which combatants learned from the harsh lessons of survival. Although there are strong similarities between the four weapons, the evidence is purely circumstantial and ignores the chief ideological difference between the AK-47 and its predecessors.

What sets the AK-47 apart is that its unfussy and robust construction facilitates mass production and a lengthy service life (typically between 6,000 and 15,000 rounds). When it went into production, the facilities used for earlier weapons were simply retooled, and the Red Army began to receive significant numbers of the AK-47 by 1956. Correctly, the version that was adopted in 1959 is titled the AKM47, with the M standing for "modern." However, despite a huge range of variants that have been produced since it first emerged, the weapon is still popularly known as the AK-47.

Arming mass infantry

The opening of the Russian front during the Second World War initiated a devastating form of conflict that had previously only been glimpsed during the Blitzkrieg attacks of 1939 to 1941, during the invasion of Poland and the Battle of France. The inhospitable and dusty steppes of summer became killing grounds of subzero intensity in the winter months. Huge encircling battles were matched against street-to-street and hand-to-hand conflicts of personal and devastating ferocity. Such a contest initiated an evolutionary leap in weapons technology at all levels. For the common soldier, though, it was in the area of hand weapons that the developments were most striking.

Three factors combined to drive a change in the hand weapons of both Axis and Soviet infantry. Firstly, the range of climatic conditions was enormous. Secondly, supply lines were massively extended, making technical repair and support a tenuous prospect. Thirdly, both sides employed vast conscript armies; basic training was swift and limited, and fighting was brutal. This meant that hand weapons had to be quickly understood and resilient. During the years from 1943 to 1945, the basic foundations of assault weapons used by modern armed forces were established.

A US Army MP inspects a captured AK-47 during the Vietnam War.

It is striking, then, that the weapon that might be considered the ultimate evolutionary product of the Russian front was not in production until the Second World War had concluded. The AK-47, created in the Soviet Union at the birth of the Cold War, was as much the product of Communist ideology as any other factor. This was a People's Weapon, democratic in the sense that it was readily useable by workers and peasants conscripted into the Red Army.

It is at this point that the AK-47 moves from assault weapon to iconic weapon. Although it is not feasible to identify any one battle or conflict in which the AK-47 played a decisive part, it has nevertheless become the best-known and most widely used gun in the world. The two factors that drove its design and production help to explain this transformation. As the standard-issue weapon of the Soviet Union, the AK-47 was distributed across Eastern Europe and allied Communist states. It was also distributed to Communist liberation movements, such as the Viet Cong. This ideological context led to the association of the AK-47 as a weapon of the people, so much so that the country of Mozambique and the organization Hezbollah both incorporate the profile of the weapon in flags and insignia. The second factor, of being useable after limited training and robust in harsh conditions, has granted the AK-47 an almost mythical status for reliability. Elite forces around the world today, such as the US Marine Corps Recon and British SAS, train with the AK-47, and pictures from Afghanistan and Iraq demonstrate the ordinary soldier's willingness to take and use the weapon.

THE AK-47

In the fiftieth year since its production, Mikhail Kalashnikov expressed regret that his invention has become probably the most significant mass-killing machine of the modern era. Millions of AK-47s have been produced on license, but many more millions were (and still are) made by unlicensed producers able to replicate a weapon that was deliberately intended for easy mass production. Gold- and chrome-plated versions of the weapon have been produced, but it is the many cheap copies that have killed millions at the hands of militias, terrorist organizations, and child soldiers around the world.

KEY FEATURE:
METAL RECEIVER

The initial design had stamped sheet-metal receivers, which proved to be a weak point. This was overcome through replacement with a heavy machined receiver adapted from an earlier Russian Mosin–Nagant rifle. These changes delayed distribution of the AK-47 to the Red Army until 1956 but were key to making it the reliable weapon that it became.

[A] Fixed butt-stock made from laminated wood

[B] Gas-chamber barrel

[C] Safety catch with three positions: safety-lock, automatic fire, and single fire

[D] Distinctive crescent-shaped magazine holding 30 rounds

[E] Adjustable iron sights, effective to 2,625 feet (800 m)

[F] Laminated-wood "cheeks"

[G] The original AK-47 had a steel pistol grip; later versions were often made of wood

[H] Fixings under the barrel can be used to attach a knife-bayonet or a 1.6-inch (40 mm) grenade launcher

KALASHNIKOV AK-47

40

Inventor(s):

Uziel Gal

UZI

Type:

Submachine gun

Social

Political

Tactical ■

Technical ■

"I'll show you my gun — my Uzi weighs a
ton/ Because I'm Public Enemy number one."

PUBLIC ENEMY, "MY UZI WEIGHS A TON"

1949

Although the two guns look markedly different, the Uzi has much in common with the Thompson (see page 138). Both were brilliantly designed and popular submachine guns, both came to have a cultural cachet with gangsters and action heroes, both became Hollywood stars in their own right, both proved their value in combat in different wars across varying theaters, and both have secured a place among the most iconic firearms of all time. Unlike the Thompson, however, the Uzi is cheap to manufacture and is still in active service around the world 60 years after its inception.

New weapon for new country

The Uzi is a submachine gun (SMG), a class of weapon called into being by the specific demands of trench warfare in the First World War, which became popular with soldiers and military tacticians as they grew to appreciate that volume of fire over a short range could be at least as important as high-powered fire capable of covering long ranges. Thus, by the end of the Second World War, the SMG was considered an indispensable element of the soldier's arsenal — perhaps even more useful and important than the traditional shoulder rifle.

Not long after the war ended, the Middle East was plunged into conflict when Israel became independent in 1948 and was promptly attacked on all sides by its Arab neighbors. The nascent Israeli Defense Force (IDF) fought off the incursion with a motley armory of war-surplus weaponry, but realized that in future conflicts — which looked inevitable — it would need a more reliable and secure supply of weapons. Accordingly, the IDF commissioned the design of a new SMG; the leading candidate was the brainchild of Lieutenant Uziel Gal, who gave his gun the first part of his name.

Gal's Uzi SMG was probably inspired by existing SMGs. The most likely inspiration is generally thought to be the Czech CZ23 and its variant the 25, also known as the Samopal 23/25, which trailed many of the Uzi's main design features. However, since the CZ23 only debuted in 1948, the year that Gal designed the Uzi, it is not clear how he could have seen it. Possibly he was aware of a prototype, or had seen British SMG prototypes with similar features.

The CZ23 fired 0.35-inch (9 mm) cartridges and featured a wraparound bolt and pistol-grip magazine, while the CZ25 had a folding metal stock. All of these became features of the Uzi. The wraparound bolt had a partly telescoping action, which meant that it enclosed one end of the barrel, shortening the overall length of the gun without making the barrel so short that it would compromise the weapon's ballistics. In a pistol-grip magazine, the magazine slots up through a hollow pistol grip, again making the weapon more compact and having the happy consequence of giving a pleasing and effective center of balance that compensates for the

natural recoil of the fast-firing mechanism, making it easier to control. The Uzi took the popular 0.35-inch (9 mm) parabellum rounds, pistol ammunition that, although not as powerful as the cartridges used in shoulder rifles like the SMLE or Springfield .30-06, had perfectly adequate stopping power over short distances. Gal's design had other advantages too; it had a robust, simple, and easy-to-produce structure with a stamped-steel body, and he designed it to intercept sand and debris before they could foul the workings, making it hard-wearing and reliable in Middle Eastern conditions.

An Israeli on guard duty in the Negev desert holds an Uzi with a fixed wooden stock.

In 1950 the IDF opted to develop Gal's Uzi, and in 1952 it was patented under his name but with manufacturing rights assigned to state-owned company Israeli Military Industries (IMI, now Israeli Weapon Industries). In 1954 the gun went into service, seeing action in the 1956 Suez campaign. The gun was issued either with a foldable wooden stock, or with the more familiar folding metal stock.

Action star

The Uzi became popular and respected by Israeli soldiers, proving its value in a succession of conflicts of existential importance for the Middle Eastern state. In the Six-Day War of 1967, the Uzi proved its value to paratroopers engaged in house-to-house fighting, the perfect environment for the compact, rapid-firing SMG. A paratrooper getting his first taste of war during the race to occupy the Old City of Jerusalem gives a vivid description of the experience of firing — and killing with — an Uzi. Coming face to face with a giant Jordanian soldier, he recalled:

> We looked at each other for half a second and I knew that it was up to me, personally, to kill him, there was no one else there. The whole thing must have lasted less than a second, but it's printed in my mind like a slow-motion movie. I fired from the hip and I can still see how the bullets splashed against the wall about a meter to his left. I moved my Uzi, slowly, slowly, it seemed, until I hit him in the body. He slipped to his knees, then he raised his head, with his face terrible, twisted in pain and hate, yes, such

Israeli soldiers on parade with their Uzis on Independence Day, 1958.

hate. I fired again and somehow got him in the head … I found I had fired my whole magazine at him.

Around the same year as the Sinai campaign, the IMI signed a deal with a Belgian manufacturer to license the Uzi. Mass production made the gun cheaper and more widely available, and it proved a huge success around the world. Over 2 million Uzis have been made, and around 10 million of its many variants or clones. There are now mini and micro Uzis, favored by secret service agents and bodyguards who provide close protection for VIPs, and international versions of the Uzi include the Socimi Type 821 (Italy), ERO (Croatia), Steyr TMP (Austria), FMK Mod 2 (Argentina), MGP-15 (Peru), Star Z-84 (Spain), and BXP and Sanna 77 (South Africa).

The fame of the gun, which means that it ranks as one of the few guns instantly recognizable around the world from its name alone, stems in part from the adoption of the Uzi and similar weapons (such as the derivative MAC-10) by gangsters and rap culture in the US. The Uzi is even more famous from its repeated appearance in Hollywood movies, perhaps most memorably in the 1984 film *The Terminator*.

UZI

41

Inventor(s):

Norman MacLeod

M18A1 CLAYMORE ANTI-PERSONNEL MINE

Social ■

Political

Tactical ■

Technical

Type:

Explosive device

"Ever courageous, never sleeps, never misses."

KHMER ROUGE GENERAL DESCRIBING THE LANDMINE

1956

The Claymore is one of the best-known, most widely produced, and most dangerous landmines in the world. It belongs to a class of weapon that, although not necessarily decisive in any one conflict, is responsible for the most widespread and enduring impact on ordinary people of almost any weapon in history.

Death from below

Mines date back to medieval siegecraft, when sappers (military engineers concerned with digging fortifications and countermeasures to fortifications) would excavate tunnels and pits beneath fortifications and enemy positions, fill them with explosives, and set them off. Landmines in the modern sense do have historical antecedents, with Chinese gunpowder-filled mines dating back to the 13th century and mechanically triggered mines deployed in the American Civil War. But it was not until the appearance of the tank at the end of the First World War that landmines became an important military consideration. The introduction of mobile armor upset the balance between offense and defense, and anti-tank mines were used in an effort to redress the balance.

These early mines were crude — often little more than wooden boxes of explosives fitted with simple pressure fuses. By the start of the Second World War, however, the Germans in particular had advanced their mine technology considerably, and this war saw the laying of hundreds of millions of mines, of two distinct

The feared German "jumping" mine, known as "Bouncing Betty" by US soldiers in the Second World War.

varieties: anti-tank and anti-personnel. The latter, defined by the Mine Ban Treaty of 1997 as "mines designed to be exploded by the presence, proximity or contact of a person and that will incapacitate, injure or kill one or more persons," were employed mainly by the Germans to impede Allied efforts to lift anti-tank mines and clear minefields. Among the most feared were the S-Mine (*Springenmine*), jumping anti-personnel mines that, when triggered, leaped up to chest height and detonated a shrapnel-filled canister with deadly effect; arguably this was the ancestor of the Claymore.

Although it was the anti-tank mines that had a greater impact in the Second World War, accounting for up to 30 percent of all tanks damaged or destroyed in the conflict, it was to be the anti-personnel mine that would leave a greater legacy in the postwar world. In the Second World War the Soviets alone were said to have laid 200 million mines, and in conflicts afterward the landmine became an important tool, not just for tactical military purposes but also to terrorize civilian populations and permanently deny access to the agricultural and economic potential of large swathes of land. Landmines became a political weapon.

Hundreds of millions were laid and vast numbers were not disposed of or even recorded properly; according to UNICEF, for instance, at least 110 million mines remain in the ground worldwide. According to the organization Landmine Monitor, 66 states and seven areas not internationally recognized are confirmed or suspected to be mine-affected. Estimating the number of people killed by mines is very difficult, but since 1975 at least a million people have been blown up by a landmine. The revulsion at the human toll of anti-personnel mines led to the adoption of the Mine Ban Treaty in 1997, to which 156 states are party. Unfortunately, they do not include most of the major military powers in the world: the US, China, India, Iran, Pakistan, Russia, and others are not signed up, although most of these have

US Marines train with the Claymore during a live-fire exercise.

stopped actively making mines. By 2012, partly as a result of the Treaty, and partly thanks to the work of mine-clearing organizations and charities, the casualty rate from landmines had dropped to around 10 casualties a day, a 60 percent decrease from 1999.

Front toward enemy

One mine that is still manufactured widely around the world is the Claymore anti-personnel mine (or derivatives of it). The mine is designed as a primarily defensive weapon to be used to cut down approaching soldiers. It is broad and shallow, with a concave surface that is aimed toward the enemy (and is famously marked in bold lettering, "Front Toward Enemy"). Inside the plastic casing is C4 explosive backing a resin matrix holding 700 steel balls, each of 0.12 inch (3 mm) diameter. Activating the fuse by electronic firing device causes the mine to explode, sending the balls blasting outward in a fan-shaped pattern that is highly lethal within a 164-foot (50 m) wide arc at 164 feet range, and has a 10 percent chance of hitting a prone man at up to 328 feet (100 m). Claymores are generally equipped with a "peep sight" on top to help the deployer line up the intended arc of explosion when setting it up.

The Claymore can trace its ancestry back to German research in the Second World War into the Misznay–Schardin effect, a phenomenon in which the blast from the face of an explosive sheet expands perpendicularly from its surface. This finding was used to design shaped charges for armor-piercing, but also proved useful to explosives researcher Norman A. MacLeod in the early 1950s as he looked to design a weapon for American soldiers to defend themselves against the "human wave" tactics adopted by the Chinese and their allies in the Korean War.

MacLeod developed the 5-pound (2.3 kg) T-48 mine in 1952, which used a shaped charge to fire steel cubes at an effective range of 40 feet (12 m); he named it the Claymore after the Scottish longsword wielded by his ancestors. In 1954 the US Army requested a lighter but more powerful version, and MacLeod collaborated with the Aerojet Corp to produce a 3.5-pound (1.6 kg) version with a 164-foot (50 m) range. This was adopted by the army in 1956 as the M18, and after safety improvements to the detonating mechanism, as the M18A1. During the Vietnam War the Claymore proved highly effective against Viet Cong and North Vietnamese opposition, who adopted human-wave assaults from their Chinese instructors, and more than 80,000 a month were churned out during the war.

The Claymore has proved popular around the world; it was even copied by the Russians during the Cold War. International variants include the Russian MON-50, the Chinese Type 66, the Vietnamese MDH-C40, and the Finnish Viuhkapanos. A smaller version, the MM-1 Minimore, is made for US Special Forces, and training versions, distinguished by their bright blue color, are made with BB pellets in place of shrapnel. These have proved popular with paintballers, and versions such as the Airsoft BB Claymore can be purchased online.

42

Inventor(s):

Wernher von Braun

INTERCONTINENTAL BALLISTIC MISSILE

Type:

Strategic nuclear-armed rocket

Social

Political ■

Tactical

Technical ■

1957

A ballistic missile is one that relies on the principles of ballistics for its trajectory and final landing point, and hence for its targeting. In a ballistic missile the launch of the missile is achieved by rocket power, but after the fuel runs out and the engine stops or is detached, the missile continues to follow a parabolic trajectory. This was the principle behind the V-2 of Wernher von Braun and the Nazi Vengeance Weapons program (see page 154), which anticipated most of the features of modern Intercontinental Ballistic Missiles (ICBMs).

Missile or rocket?

Technically, a missile is any object that travels through the air, from a stone hurled by a caveman to an arrow fired from a composite bow. In modern military parlance, however, "missile" generally refers to a guided self-propelled weapon, whereas a rocket is an unguided self-propelled weapon. These distinctions are easily blurred — most missiles are rockets in terms of their propulsion method, and ICBMs have evolved from being unguided rockets to having very high-precision guidance systems.

The V-2 was a single-stage, relatively small rocket, and could achieve a peak altitude of only around 60 miles (97 km) and hence a maximum range of only about 200 miles (322 km). Modern ICBMs have multiple stages and planet-circling range. The Minuteman 3, for instance, the current frontline ICBM for the US, travels at speeds of up to Mach 23 (15,000 mph/ 24,140 kph), reaching a height of up to 700 miles (1,127 km) above Earth, almost three times higher than the orbit of the International Space Station, and a range of over 6,000 miles (9,656 km).

A US airman inspects a Minuteman III ICBM in its silo in the late 1980s.

The Missile Gap

In the aftermath of the Second World War, the Americans were shocked at how quickly the Soviet Union developed its own nuclear weapons, but remained complacent about their superiority in bomber capacity, and thus in their ability to prevail in a nuclear confrontation with the Soviets. In 1957, however, the USSR successfully launched the first ICBM, using rocket technology partly derived from captured elements of the Nazi V-2 program. Later that year they used the same rockets to propel *Sputnik* (a relatively heavy payload) and then Laika the dog into space. The Americans realized that they had neglected rocket development and that the Soviets now possessed a first-strike capacity that potentially overmatched their own. The US government was gripped by a "Missile Gap" panic, and the American rocket program, helmed by Wernher von Braun himself, was accelerated. On the election trail in 1960, John F. Kennedy proclaimed, "Control of space will be decided in the next decade. If the Soviets control space

An Atlas missile test launch at Cape Canaveral in 1958; the Atlas was the first US ICBM.

"At a small United States Air Force installation in eastern Wyoming, I'm sitting at an electronic console, ready to unleash nuclear hell. In front of me is a strange amalgamation of '60s-era flip switches and modern digital display screens. It's the control console for launching an intercontinental ballistic missile or ICBM."

JOHN NOONAN, CAPTAIN USAF, ASSIGNED TO THE 321ST MISSILE SQUADRON IN CHEYENNE, WYOMING; "IN NUCLEAR SILOS, DEATH WEARS A SNUGGIE," *WIRED.COM*, 2011

TYPES OF BALLISTIC MISSILE

Not all ballistic missiles (BM) are intercontinental. The chart below shows the types of BM and their ranges:

Type	Acronym	Range
Battlefield range	BRBM	Less than 124 miles (200 km)
Tactical	TAC	93–186 miles (150–300 km)
Short range	SRBM	Less than 621 miles (1,000 km)
Theater	TBM	186–2,175 miles (300–3,500 km)
Medium range	MRBM	621–2,175 miles (1,000–3,500 km)
Intermediate range or long range	IRBM or LRBM	2,175–3,418 miles (3,500–5,500 km)
Intercontinental	ICBM	More than 3,418 miles (5,500 km)

they can control Earth, as in the past centuries the nations that controlled the seas dominated the continents."

By this time Lockheed Martin had already developed the first American ICBM rocket, the single-stage Atlas D, operational in 1959, together with the reentry vehicles that carried the nuclear warhead back down into the Earth's atmosphere after the rocket stage had dropped away. At the same time they had begun work on the Titan ICBM, a two-stage ICBM that went into service between 1962 and 1965, when it was replaced by the Titan II. Whereas the Atlas and Titan I had used cryogenically cooled liquid propellant, which was dangerous and difficult to store and could only be loaded into the rockets just before launch (making rapid launch impossible), the Titan II used noncryogenic, storable propellant. The Minuteman missiles that came later used solid propellants,

permanently housed in the body of the missile, meaning they could be launched within minutes. The other major advances, alongside propellants and range, were ever-increasing accuracy and the introduction of multiple independent reentry vehicles (MIRVs), which meant that one missile could launch multiple warheads at multiple, widely spaced targets.

A Titan II ICBM is launched at Vandenberg Air Force Base in California, 1975.

Gerald Ford and Leonid Brezhnev sign an arms
limitation treaty in 1974.

MAD world

The strategic consequences of nuclear-armed
ICBMs were profound. At first the superpowers
built their forces around attaining superior
first-capacity, but it soon became apparent that
each side had more than enough missiles to
wipe out the other, even as part of a secondary,
retaliatory strike capacity. This was assured
when submarines were armed with ICBMs,
such as the Polaris missile introduced in 1961,
which meant that there was no way to eradicate
the other side's retaliatory strike capacity.

Under Kennedy, the sheer destructive
power of the warheads possessed by each side
led to the formulation of the doctrine of
mutually assured destruction (MAD), part of a
wider doctrine of deterrence, with ICBMs as the
essential tool to deter both the enemy from
attacking — as he would then face apocalyptic
retaliation — and one's own side from attacking,
as the enemy possessed the same capacity. Since
each side already possessed enough firepower to
achieve MAD, a natural limit was reached on
the need for further nuclear weapon

development. Talks between the superpowers
led to the Strategic Arms Limitation Talks
(SALT) and the Strategic Arms Reduction
Treaty (START), and the end of the Cold War
saw a further diminution in the need for
ICBMs. Nonetheless, the number of states with
ICBM capacity remains high, and lesser ballistic
missiles capable of reaching across continents
are or have been possessed by states such as
Iran, Iraq, Israel, and North Korea.

Always ready to spring

One peculiar consequence of the ICBM was the
need to build hidden, first-strike-proof launch
silos, staffed with crew on constant alert to
launch a nuclear strike at a moment's notice. The
doctrine of deterrence simultaneously assumed
that these crews would never be required to act,
at the same time depending on their infallible
readiness to do so. In his 1959 book, *Strategy in
the Missile Age*, Bernard Brodie pointed to the
difficulties inherent in this set-up: "We expect
the system to be always ready to spring while
going permanently unused."

Life in the silos became a strange existence, tedious but stressful, quiet but extremely dangerous. Earlier ICBMs, such as the Titan IIs, in service from 1964 to 1987, were accident-prone and fragile. In one incident a technician dropped a wrench on a Titan stored in a silo near Damascus, Arkansas, causing a fuel leak and explosion that blew the warhead out of the silo, fortunately without setting it off.

The military science

Ballistics — the study of the course of projectiles, and by extension the science of motion — has come to be the most important intersection between weapons and science. From a military point of view it has been essential in guiding development of more accurate and effective weapons, from early cannons to the apotheosis of ballistic weaponry, the ICBM. Its importance is arguably even greater from the perspective of science, since the pursuit of ballistics, beginning with the interest in artillery of mathematicians such as Niccolò Tartaglia, led directly to the epochal work of Galileo on falling bodies and thence to Newton's theory of gravity and the advent of the scientific revolution.

A Polaris missile on the launch pad at Cape Canaveral during testing of the weapon, which became most important as a submarine-launched missile.

43

Inventor(s):

Eugene Stoner

M16 RIFLE

Type:

Assault rifle

Social

Political ■

Tactical

Technical ■

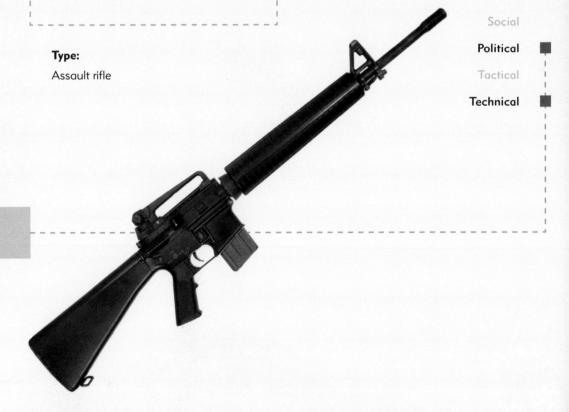

1959

The M16, in one form or another, is the standard-issue service rifle for almost all branches of the US military. Generally regarded as one of the finest assault rifles in the world, technically superior to the AK-47, the M16 and its variants are the longest-serving general-issue rifles in American military history. Yet this weapon has had the most troubled history and reputation of almost any rifle of the last hundred years, and it is still beset by contention more than 50 years after its invention.

The black rifle

The origins of the M16 lay in an intense debate within the US military in the aftermath of the Korean War. Reports commissioned by the Operations Research Office (ORO), set up by the US Army, concluded that most successful hits achieved by American soldiers were at short range and not really the result of careful aiming, and that the best way for the average soldier to improve his or her chance of scoring a hit was to replace single, heavy-caliber shots with multiple, lower-caliber shots. Acting on these conclusions would require a revision of prevailing US Army principles of rifle design, and replacement of the newly developed service rifle, the M14, a descendant of the M1 Garand (see page 146).

One solution was developed by Eugene Stoner at the Armalite weapons manufacturer. His AR-15 fired a relatively small caliber bullet, a .22 caliber (5.56 x 45 mm), but one that used new powder formulation to achieve colossal muzzle velocity. Whereas the 7.62 mm fired by the M14 had a muzzle velocity of 933 yards per second (853 m/s), the .22 caliber traveled at 1,094 yards per second (1,000 m/s). Since kinetic energy is disproportionately dependent on velocity over

mass, this faster projectile offered extremely high penetrating power despite its reduced mass, whereas the small, lightweight ammo meant that the soldier could carry more into combat and squeeze more into each cartridge. To fire these new bullets, Stoner designed a lightweight, futuristic gun, with plastic furniture that led to its being dubbed "the black gun."

The new rifle had many advantages: it was easier to fire and to fire accurately, thanks to the lower recoil associated with the smaller bullets, making it easier for a range of physical types to use. The configuration of the gun combined with the lower recoil to make it easier to stay on target, even when firing on full-auto. Crucially, it was much lighter than its main competitor: the AR-15 rifle, with 120 rounds of ammunition, weighed just 11.1 pounds (5 kg)compared to the M-14's 18.75 pounds (8.5 kg). When prototype AR-15s were sent to Vietnam for field testing by South Vietnamese forces in 1962, the positive reports helped convince the US Army to dump the M14 and adopt the AR-15 instead, rechristening it the M16. It became the standard US Army rifle in 1967.

Failure to extract

Unfortunately, the military horribly botched the rollout of the new weapon, thanks to cost-cutting measures. The powder used in the gun's ammunition was replaced with a cheaper, dirtier version that left more residue, and protective but expensive chrome-plating of important working parts was dropped. Colt, which had acquired the rights to the design in 1959, had aggressively marketed it as a low-maintenance, "self-cleaning" gun, and accordingly no cleaning kits were issued with the new rifle and there was no training in cleaning. Yet this was the crucial flaw in the M16, which proved to suffer a terribly high rate of jamming, especially the worst sort of jam, known as "failure to extract," where a spent cartridge refuses to dislodge from the chamber after firing. The best way to clear such a jam was to stick a rod down the muzzle of the barrel; in the words of *The New York Times*, "The modern American assault rifle, in other words, often resembled a single-shot musket." According to previously classified Army records from 1967, 80 percent of 1,585 troops queried in 1967 had experienced a stoppage while firing.

The other serious and persisting gripe pertaining to the M16 was its perceived lack of stopping power. The light-caliber bullets had so much kinetic energy that they could penetrate enemy bulletproofing, but when hitting lightly clothed enemies, such as US soldiers have often faced from Vietnam to Iraq to Afghanistan, the bullets often pass straight through like a laser.

There was such an outcry about the problems experienced with the early M16 that a Congressional inquiry was held and remedies were swiftly applied. Cleaner powder was used and chrome-plating of vital parts reintroduced. Troops were trained to clean their rifles and issued with cleaning kits. By the end of the Vietnam war the M16A1 was a mature and reliable weapon. In 1983 it was superseded by the M16A2, which had a heavier barrel with improved flash-suppressor and better sights, and which could support a grenade-launcher attachment. This in turn has been superseded by the M16A4, which has rails for easy attachment and detachment of adaptations such as night-vision sights. The carbine (i.e., shorter and lighter version), known as the M4, is also extremely popular and widely used in the US military, and the M16-type rifle has been adopted by over 40 countries to date. Over 10 million M16s and derivatives have been manufactured since 1959, with the design licensed to at least eight different manufacturers at one time or another. Yet controversy still dogs the rifle.

Ill repute

Its reputation for jamming and lack of stopping power persists. For instance, according to the anonymous Marine calling himself "Semper Fi," writing in 2005 after a tour of duty in Iraq, the M16 gets a thumbs down:

> Chronic jamming problems with the talcum powder like sand over there. The sand is everywhere … The M-4 carbine version is more popular because it's lighter and shorter, but it has jamming problems also. They like the ability to mount the various optical gunsights and weapons lights on the … rails, but the weapon itself is

not great in a desert environment. They all hate the 5.56 mm (.223) round. Poor penetration on the cinderblock structure common over there and even torso hits can't be reliably counted on to put the enemy down.

This report is typical of continuing public perception of the M16, yet careful investigation by the military casts doubt on the factual basis of this bad reputation. A survey by the Center for Naval Analysis in 2006 found that 75 percent of soldiers reported overall satisfaction with the M16 and 89 percent with the M4. And although this survey also found that 19 percent of the soldiers had experienced "a stoppage while engaging the enemy," army tests, involving firing more than 8 million rounds through M4s, found that the average stoppage rate was less than once per 3,600 rounds (equivalent to 120 magazines

of ammunition, more than many soldiers fire in an entire combat tour). According to Colonel Douglas Tamilio, supervisor of M4 development for the Army Materiel Command, the reliability of M16 derivatives is "on par with any assault rifle in the world … The data suggests we don't have a systematic problem. The reliability issues we are hearing [come] from non-soldiers." One of the great strengths of the M16 is that its design is highly flexible, making it a robust and proven platform for constant updating and improvement. For instance, Tamilio points out that since its introduction in the early 1990s the M4 carbine has had over 62 improvements to its design.

M16 RIFLE

44

Inventor(s):

Soviet Army

RPG-7 ROCKET-PROPELLED GRENADE LAUNCHER

Type:

Anti-armor weapon

Social

Political ■

Tactical ■

Technical

1961

The RPG-7 is the most successful rocket grenade launcher ever; more than 50 years after its debut it continues to see active service in over 50 countries, as well as being the preferred weapon for a host of terrorist and insurgent groups. This relatively simple weapon has had profound geopolitical consequences as a key element in asymmetric warfare. Yet the one thing that most people think they know about it is wrong. "RPG" does not, originally at least, stand for "rocket-propelled grenade," but for the Russian phrase *ruchnoi protivotankovy granatamyot* (handheld anti-tank grenade-launcher).

Anti-tank

The advent of tanks in the First World War helped to break the deadlock of trench warfare and threatened to permanently upset the balance between armor and infantry. Effective mobile armor demanded a response, and although the Germans scrambled to improvise one in the First World War, using heavy bolt-action rifles, by the Second World War there was a more comprehensive menu of anti-tank options. One way to breach armor was through sheer kinetic energy — i.e., by firing something fast and heavy enough to punch through armor; this required a heavy weapon. The other main way was to use explosives designed specifically to pierce armor on impact; on detonation, hollow, shaped charges with metal lining would focus their explosive energy on driving the now molten metal into a piercing, needlelike stream or jet. This is the method still employed in high explosive anti-tank (HEAT) rounds today.

Shaped HEAT rounds could be delivered by relatively light grenades, making it possible to develop man-portable grenade delivery systems. Rockets were favored for these weapons because

they are self-propelling and hence do not generate recoil in the launcher. The Americans had success with the bazooka, the British with the PIAT and the Germans, leading the way, with the Panzerfaust. The Panzerfaust was relatively cheap and simple to make and easy to operate, and was liberally distributed to all German forces. Individual infantrymen now had the firepower to take out tanks. The

A British officer examines a captured German Panzerfaust anti-tank weapon, at Anzio in 1944.

A soldier from the Afghan National Army trains with the RPG-7 in 2013; the RPG-7 is so familiar in the Afghan theater of war that the National Army adopted it as official issue.

Russians initially had no answer to the Panzerfaust, but they adapted the German design to create a series of RPG grenade launchers, culminating in the RPG-7, introduced in 1961.

Tube travel

A rocket grenade launcher is essentially a tube to hold the rocket grenade in place and give it enough direction on launch to achieve some measure of accuracy. It needs a trigger to set off the rocket grenade, and must be open at the back to allow exhaust gases to vent. It may be fitted with sights, or have mounts for more advanced optics such as night-vision sights. The RPG-7 ingeniously solves the main problem facing rocket grenade launcher designers: dealing with the rocket exhaust. The purpose of the weapon is to be portable, so the launch tube must be as short as possible, but it must also be long enough for the rocket motor to have burnt all its fuel by the time it exits the tube, or its exhaust will burn the operator's face. In the RPG-7, the rocket grenades are fitted with a small "booster" charge that throws the rocket grenade clear of the launch tube at about 384 feet per second (117 m/s); this acceleration sets off a piezoelectric (pressure-generated spark)

"The RPG: Probably the infantry weapon most feared by our guys. Simple, reliable and as common as dogshit."

Marine "Semper Fi," 2005, describing conditions in Iraq

fuse attached to the rocket "sustainer" motor, which then ignites, accelerating the projectile to 965 feet per second (294 m/s) and carrying it to its target. The sustainer motor does not kick in until the rocket grenade is 12 yards (11 m) clear of the launcher, thus protecting the operator, although he still has to be aware that exhaust gases from the booster charge will vent from the back of the tube. Range depends on the type of grenade launched but can be up to 165 yards (150 m). Even fitted with a telescopic sight the launch tube itself weighs just 14.3 pounds (6.3 kg), and can be reused, making it attractive to cash-strapped irregular forces.

Armor penetration

In 1961 the RPG-7b was typically loaded with PG-7V HEAT grenades, which could penetrate about 10 inches (254 mm) of armor. Armored vehicles responded by increasing the thickness of their armor, and an arms race developed that continues to this day. Modern RPGs are typically used with PG-7M warheads, which can penetrate up to 11.8 inches (300 mm) of armor, whereas the PG-7VR, introduced in 1988, has a dual explosive head to defeat explosive reactive armor (ERA): the first charge sets off the ERA, and the second one can penetrate up to 24 inches (610 mm) of armor. Other types of grenades are used for anti-infantry and anti-bunker use.

The RPG-7 is cheap, robust, simple to operate, and widely available. Many fighting forces, including terror and insurgent groups, face the problem of asymmetric warfare: fighting a war against opponents whose technological and logistical capacity dwarfs their own. Insurgents in the Iraq War, for instance, were up against highly trained, heavily armed US soldiers with artillery and air support on hand, equipped with armored vehicles. Alongside the AK-47 and the IED (see pages 166 and 204), the RPG is the solution to this problem. It enables a single man to knock out armor, and possibly even to down close-air support helicopters. The ubiquity of RPGs has become a vital tactical and strategic consideration in the asymmetric warfare that characterizes so many modern conflicts. In Iraq, for instance, the RPG was second only to IEDs as a cause of casualties inflicted on US forces.

Reports from the front line of the recent conflict in Iraq graphically drive home the "shoot and scoot" fighting that characterizes RPG deployment. A Marine nicknaming himself "Semper Fi," describing conditions in an email to his father in 2005, described the RPG as "Probably the infantry weapon most feared by our guys. Simple, reliable and as common as dogshit. The enemy responded to our up-armored humvees by aiming at the windshields, often at point blank range. Still killing a lot of our guys."

45

Inventor(s):
General Dynamics Land Systems

M1 ABRAMS TANK

Type:

Main battle tank

Social

Political ■

Tactical ■

Technical

"The M1 is an extraordinary vehicle, the best tank on the planet."

ARMY MAJOR GENERAL (RET) PAUL D. EATON, NATIONAL SECURITY NETWORK

1980

The M1 Abrams tank is the main battle tank of the US and several other nations including Egypt and Saudi Arabia. Known as "the Beast," "Whispering Death," and "Dracula," in reference to its awesome killing power and relatively quiet operation, the Abrams has gone through several updates, with the original M1 giving way to the M1A1 and then the M1A2. This in turn has been updated using system enhancement packages (SEPs). The most up-to-date version of the tank is the M1A2SEPv2. Over 8,800 M1 and M1A1 tanks were built, along with hundreds of M1A2s, and hundreds of older models have been upgraded to the most recent specifications.

Gas-guzzling beast

Although the Abrams is widely regarded as the best tank in the world, and has proved itself unmatched in its primary battlefield role as a tank killer, it is increasingly mired in controversy over its economic, political, and social dimensions, while simultaneously beset by doubts over its future role and long-term relevance. The travails of the M1 Abrams reveal a great deal about both the future of tanks and the nature of future warfare in general.

The Abrams is superior in almost every aspect of tank design and function. It is incredibly powerful, fast, and maneuverable; heavily armored and protected; bristling with high-powered armaments; and equipped with state-of-the-art fire-control systems. At the core of the tank is its gas turbine engine. Gas turbine engines give higher power to weight ratios than normal reciprocating engines. The M1A1 had a Honeywell AGT 1500 gas turbine engine, with Allison X-1100-3B transmission to provide four forward and two reverse gears. The M1A2 has an upgraded LV100-5 gas turbine engine; this is quiet and produces no visible exhaust (helping to reduce risk of detection), yet is capable of

accelerating from 0 to 20 mph (0–32 kph) in 7.2 seconds, safely traveling at 30 mph (48 kph) even going cross-country, according to General Dynamics Land Systems. Where the engine falls down is in fuel consumption: despite its advanced digital fuel-control system, it achieves less than one mile per gallon. To get a decent range the tank must be fitted with colossal fuel tanks, with a full load of 490 gallons (1,855 l). Abrams can go 265 miles (426 km) before refuelling.

The M1A1 sported advanced ceramic armor, whereas the A2 has upped the ante still further by incorporating depleted (nonradioactive) uranium, which is more than 2.5 times denser than steel. This helps raise the total weight of the tank to 73 tons (65 tonnes). The Abrams also has reactive armor tiles, designed to counterattack the armor-piercing mechanism of HEAT rounds (see page 191), as well as smoke-screen generating capabilities.

The main armament is the mighty Rheinmetall M256 120 mm smoothbore cannon, which can level a building from a range

View from above as an Abrams tank fires its 120 mm cannon.

when the initial "sabot" casing of the round drops away after firing, concentrating all the kinetic energy of the shot into the penetrator).

The Abrams' cannon can pierce the armor of any current opposing tank; it has a higher hit/kill ratio than any other main battle tank. What makes it particularly fearsome is the advanced fire-control systems that acquire and impact targets. Adaptations such as thermal imaging and integrated battlefield communications (which pull together information from sources as diverse as satellite imagery, other tanks, intelligence reports, radar, and so on) help the tank to find targets from long range, and the tank's unusual ability to compensate for the effects of travel over rough terrain mean that, unlike most tanks, it can fire accurately while on the move.

Trial by fire

The M1 Abrams was developed by 1978 and entered service in 1980, but did not see action for over a decade. The Gulf War of 1991 saw almost 2,000 M1A1s deployed in theater, but there were widespread concerns about how the relatively untested tank would stand up to the rigors of desert combat and the threat of Iraqi armor, which included some of the most up-to-date Soviet tanks. In the event the M1A1 passed the test with flying colors. Only 18 of the tanks had to be withdrawn from service, and according to some accounts not a single one was due to enemy tank fire; it turned out that the only tank the Abrams had to fear was other Abrams, with seven destroyed by friendly fire. Nonetheless, not a single Abrams crewman was

of 2.5 miles (4 km). The smoothbore reduces accuracy, but allows for a faster muzzle velocity, which adds power to the armor-piercing rounds fired, particularly the sabot rounds (where a dense, heavy, needlelike depleted-uranium "penetrator" is accelerated to very high velocity

lost in the conflict and the Abrams maintained 90 percent operational readiness.

Although the Abrams again saw service in the Iraq War of 2003, and again proved practically invulnerable to conventional anti-tank weapons, the subsequent insurgency and conflicts have raised serious questions about the long-term utility of the model, and perhaps of tank warfare itself. The primary role of the main battle tank is to take out other tanks, and tanks in general make most sense in the context of a conflict between conventional armies, each equipped with armor and organized forces. The problem is that even the US military does not foresee this context arising again. "We don't believe we'll ever see a straight conventional conflict again in the future," Army Chief of Staff Ray Odierno told a Congressional hearing in early 2012. Instead, what faces Western forces, including the Abrams tank, is unconventional, guerrilla, and asymmetric warfare, where the enemy has little or no armor, there are no tank battles, few open battlefields, and the enemy attacks using IEDs and RPGs. In Iraq and Afghanistan, for instance, the Abrams suffered extensively from IED attacks, which struck at the bottom of the vehicle where its armor is most vulnerable. Many Abrams in Iraq ended up in a similar state to the heavy Tiger tanks of late Second World War Germany: dug in as extremely expensive pillboxes.

The home front

It is in this context that the Abrams has found itself at the center of a storm of controversy that has little to do with the battlefield. Seeking to achieve massive reductions in its spending, the Pentagon had identified the program of continued upgrade of Abrams tanks to the latest M1A2SEPv2 configuration as unnecessary, and announced its intention to suspend the program for around four years, starting in late 2013. The decision seemed reasonable, given that, at the time of writing, there are nearly 2,400 Abrams deployed around the world, of which around two-thirds have been upgraded (and are, on average, effectively three years old or less), whereas another 3,000 older models are parked at a military base in California.

Abrams tank production, however, is an example of how a weapon can have social, economic, and political impacts unrelated to its battlefield performance. General Dynamics, who make the tank, estimated in 2011 that across the US the Abrams program involves more than 560 subcontractors employing 18,000 people. Spending millions of dollars in campaign contributions and on a feverish lobbying campaign, the company succeeded in convincing lawmakers to fend off the Pentagon's proposed cuts, and, at the time of writing, the upgrade program was set to continue.

46

Inventor(s):

Raytheon

BGM-109 TOMAHAWK CRUISE MISSILE

Type:

Long-range missile

Social

Political ■

Tactical

Technical ■

1983

A cruise missile is a self-guiding, self-propelling missile capable of hitting very precise targets from long range (over 1,000 miles/1,609 km). It cruises along a flat trajectory, generating lift with a turbofan engine and stubby wings. Because it travels at very low altitude and has a very small cross-section its radar profile is almost nonexistent, making it very hard to defend against. Accordingly, the cruise missile has proved to be a potent solution to one of the greatest problems facing democratic nations in the exercise of military power, particularly when not acting directly in defense of the nation: public reluctance to accept the human cost of war.

Vengeance and loons

Traditionally, military planners had to choose between very imprecise attacks launched from long enough range to protect their forces from risk of harm, with attendant risk of high collateral damage (notably civilian casualties) due to the lack of precision, and high-precision attacks launched from very close range (i.e., by "boots on the ground"), with attendant risks to military personnel. The cruise missile is the flag-bearer for a new kind of weapon: publically and politically acceptable unmanned weapons with high enough precision to minimize civilian casualties.

The first cruise missile was the groundbreaking German V-1 (see page 154), which closely resembles its modern descendants in basic layout and concept. The US Navy used V-1 technology acquired from the Germans to build the first American cruise missile, the Loon, shortly after the Second World War, and this was followed by the Regulus I, developed in 1953. The Regulus was deployed with the submarine fleet in the mid-1950s but development was halted in 1958 after it was decided to pursue the Polaris ballistic missile program. In the 1970s improvements in technology revived the cruise missile concept, and the Raytheon Company developed the BGM-109 Tomahawk Land Attack Missile (TLAM), which entered service with the US Navy in 1983. There are other types of cruise missile but the Tomahawk is by far the most successful.

Tomahawks are 20.5 feet (6.25 m) long and 1.7 feet (0.52 m) across. At launch they are blasted clear of the launch vehicle (originally submarines, but now mainly surface ships) by a solid rocket booster, which makes up 551 pounds (250 kg) of the missile's overall weight of 3,197 pounds (1,450 kg). Once the fuel is burned up the booster falls away and the turbofan engine takes over; it weighs just 143 pounds (65 kg) but delivers 600 pounds (272 kg) of thrust. Cruising at 550 mph (885 kph), the missile has a range of 1,000 miles (1,609 km) or more.

Key to the precision of the Tomahawk is the guidance system. Early models used a combination of inertial guidance, where the

" ... the building was hit by the cruise missile last night. It had two gaping holes ... It was obviously completely ruined, a several stories high building just completely ruined. Another building at the back ... was smoldering. These things are just awesome when they hit something. They really do some damage."

IAN MCPHEDRAN, NEWS LTD CORRESPONDENT, INTERVIEWED FROM BAGHDAD ON ABC'S *7.30 REPORT*, MARCH 2003

missile computes the course covered through measuring changes in acceleration (a form of dead reckoning), and TERCOM (terrain contour matching), where the missile compares the profile of the terrain over which it is passing with prerecorded contour maps. More recent models have used GPS and DSMAC (digital scene matching area correlation), where the missile's computer compares a stored image of the target with the image coming live from the onboard camera.

This combination of systems allows Tomahawks to perform impressive feats of navigation and accuracy. When it reaches its target, the Tomahawk can deliver one of two warheads: a 1,000 lb (454 kg) conventional warhead, or a submunitions dispenser, which scatters up to 166 armor-piercing, fragmentation, or incendiary bomblets in 24 packages. Previously, some cruise missiles were fitted with W80 nuclear warheads, but this is no longer the case.

Desert strikes

The cruise missile has proved itself in the 1990s and since as one of the most important weapons in the American arsenal (the UK has also bought Tomahawks). It was first deployed, to devastating effect, in the Persian Gulf War of 1991, during Operation Desert Storm. It played a key role in the initial air strikes degrading Iraqi operational and air defense capacity, when it was the only weapon used during daylight hours. Over 280 Tomahawks were fired from submarines and surface ships. The missile bombardment of Baghdad achieved a high level of precision, and also dealt a crushing blow to the morale of the citizens. Shortly after leaving Baghdad in January 1991, BBC producer Anthony Massey told the *Los Angeles Times*: "The city appears virtually undamaged because of the accuracy of the cruise missile ... but it is completely deserted. This is really the final straw [for the residents] ... They're leaving as fast as they can."

In Desert Storm, the Tomahawk showed what it was capable of, but it also suffered from a higher degree of operational failures than was admitted at the time. Since then, the Mk III and Mk IV versions have greatly improved accuracy. The Mk III was first used in September 1995 in the Deliberate Force operation strike on Bosnia, and again in the September 1996 Iraq operation, Desert Strike; in both cases the success rate of

the missile was above 90 percent, and over its whole operational life the Tomahawk has a greater than 85 percent success rate.

The Mk IV Tomahawk was deployed against Colonel Gadhafi's forces in Libya in 2011; more than 230 were launched, with one submarine alone firing over 90 of the missiles. According to Rear Admiral William Shannon III, the cruise missiles ensured the success of the NATO air campaign, "because Tomahawk was there first and took out most of the air defense systems and most of the aircraft that were sitting on the airfields."

The Tomahawk IV can be redirected mid-flight, and can transmit real-time imagery to its controllers, making it more flexible and easier to target. It can even be directed to circle until a target is determined, and the US Navy is working on partnering Tomahawk IVs with unmanned aerial vehicles (UAVs) — technically speaking, a cruise missile is a UAV, just a one-way version — to form remotely operated hunter–killer teams. Such high-tech firepower does not come cheap. Each Tomahawk costs about $1.4 million, according to government budget documents. October 2013 saw the 3,000th Tomahawk IV delivered to the US Navy, whereas the NATO operation in Libya saw the 2,000th combat firing of a Tomahawk. Cruise missiles may offer a relatively "clean" means of waging war, but what they save in blood they make up for in treasure.

A Tomahawk Land-Attack Missile is fired at an Iraqi target from the *USS Mississippi* during Operation Desert Storm.

47

Inventor(s):

USAF

SMART BOMB

Type:

Precision-guided munitions

Social

Political

Tactical

Technical

Late 20th-century

"Smart bomb" is the colloquial name for a laser-guided bomb, perhaps the most important type of precision-guided munition (PGM). PGMs, and smart bombs in particular, have revolutionized the calculus of air war — and military engagement in general — at every level: political, strategic, operational, tactical, and economic.

Off target

In the past, the accuracy of bombing raids was appalling, and collateral damage so inevitable that it was adopted as the primary purpose of the raids. In late 1944, for instance, just 7 percent of all bombs dropped by the US Eighth Air Force landed within 985 feet (300 m) of their target. To guarantee a 96 percent chance that just two bombs would land inside a German power plant that measured 400 by 500 feet (122 x 152 m), required 108 B-17 bombers crewed by 1,080 airmen to drop 648 bombs. Accuracy of munitions is quantified using the circular error probable (CEP), the radius of the circle within which 50 percent of munitions can be expected to land. In the Second World War, to achieve a 90 percent chance of hitting a 60 by 100 foot (18 x 30 m) target using "dumb" (i.e., unguided) 2,000-pound (907 kg) bombs dropped from medium altitude, required over 9,070 bombs (3,024 plane loads), with a CEP of 3,300 feet (roughly 1 km). In other words, an area 1.2 miles (2 km) across could expect to be devastated, and the lives of over 3,000 bomber crews endangered, without even guaranteeing a hit on a relatively large target. By the Vietnam

War, it still required 176 dumb bombs to achieve the same hit rate, with a CEP of 400 feet (122 m). Even when released by smart bombers, dumb bombs are incapable of achieving high levels of precision.

A bridge too far

Such a reckless waste of collateral casualties, aircrew, aircraft, and munitions called for urgent remedy, and attempts were made to introduce PGMs from early on. On May 12th, 1943, an RAF Liberator dropped an acoustic homing torpedo that damaged its U-boat target sufficiently to drive it to the surface where it was destroyed: this may be the first successful PGM strike. Four months later a German Dornier bomber dropped a radio-controlled glide bomb that sank an Italian battleship. By the end of the war a variety of guidance technologies had been trialed, including radio, radar, and even television, whereas Kamikaze tactics had shown that in-flight targeting of a projectile up to impact could achieve devastating results. Approximately 34 US

Navy ships were sunk by Kamikaze attacks, and 368 others damaged; nearly 8.5 percent of all ships hit by Kamikazes sank.

One of the toughest targets to hit with dumb bombs is a bridge, and after the Second World War PGMs would prove their value in bridge bombing. In the Korean War Razon and Tarzon guided bombs successfully destroyed at least 19 North Korean bridges. But the US Air Force's concentration on the development of nuclear weapons saw PGMs sidelined, and it was not until the 1960s that there was a belated awareness that nonnuclear warfare still required new approaches. In the mid-1960s the Air Force developed the laser-guided bomb (LGB), which could achieve an astonishing CEP of just 20 feet (6 m), even in its early forms. The laser-guided smart bomb was first field-tested in 1968, but had to wait until 1972 for a definitive demonstration of its capabilities. The Thanh Hoa bridge in North Vietnam, a vital strategic target, had proven almost immune to dumb bombing raids, with repeated attacks costing many aircraft and their crew. On May 13th, 1972, four flights of F-4 Phantoms armed with LGBs took out the bridge with relative ease — this is often said to mark the start of the PGM era. Over the following months smart bombs were used to devastating effect in Operation Linebacker, a bombing campaign that inflicted massive damage on North Vietnamese attempts to launch a mechanized invasion, and were instrumental in forcing the North Vietnamese leadership to come to the bargaining table.

Surgical strikes

It was in the first Gulf War, during Operation Desert Storm, that smart bombs came of age. Although just 4.3 percent of the munitions expended by American air strikes were LGBs, they accounted for around 75 percent of the serious damage inflicted on strategic and operational targets. For example, in the course of a four-week bombing campaign PGMs took out 41 of 54 strategically vital Iraqi bridges and 31 of the pontoon bridges constructed to replace them. Similar lethal accuracy was achieved against command and control structures and, particularly, Iraqi armor and vehicles. An Iraqi general interviewed after the war reflected: "During the Iran war, my tank was my friend because I could sleep in it and know I was safe ... During this war my tank became my enemy ...

"Desert Storm reconfirmed that Laser-Guided Bombs possessed a near single-bomb target-destruction capability, an unprecedented if not revolutionary development in aerial warfare."

GULF WAR AIR POWER SURVEY, 1993

none of my troops would get near a tank at night because they just kept blowing up."

PGMs performed even better during Operation Deliberate Force, the NATO air campaign against Serbian forces in 1995. Thanks largely to PGMs, which accounted for 69 percent of the weapons used by NATO forces, the operation's objectives were achieved. Former Assistant Secretary of State Richard Holbrooke later noted: "One of the great things that people should have learned from this is that there are times when air power — not backed up by ground troops — can make a difference."

As well as saving lives on both sides of a conflict by reducing collateral damage and enabling fewer sorties, which can launch munitions from further away, PGMs can save money. For instance, a cruise missile is from 16 to 60 times more expensive than a smart bomb. The cost (at the time) of the smart bombs dropped by F-117As in the Gulf War was around $146 million; to deliver the same tonnage of explosives by Tomahawk (see page 196) would have cost $4.8 billion.

DARPA dreams

Smart bombs and PGMs in general are one of the research priorities of the US government's Defense Advanced Research Projects Agency (DARPA). Currently, DARPA is working on a host of technologies with exotic and obscure codenames or acronyms such as EXACTO, DuDE, PINS, and PGK. These aim to miniaturize advanced guidance and sensor technologies (for instance, with the ability to calculate course through minute changes in acceleration, or pick up very faint laser reflections), with a view to applying them to munitions of every kind, from large bombs to artillery shells, and maybe even to bullets fired by individual soldiers. "There is kind of a metatrend in navigation," notes US Air Force Lt. Col. Jay Lowell of DARPA, "the democratization of high-end technologies into a broader set of applications. In this case, doing what had been reserved for high-end systems on smaller munitions available in greater numbers … the idea of moving precision navigation to be better and more broadly used is really the cornerstone."

A test version of a hi-tech new multirole combat aircraft, the Joint Strike Fighter, drops a hi-tech laser-guided "smart bomb."

48

Inventor(s):

Insurgents

IMPROVISED EXPLOSIVE
DEVICE (IED)

Type:

Anti-personnel and vehicle explosive

Social ■

Political

Tactical ■

Technical

21st century

An improvised explosive device (IED) can be a bomb, mine, grenade, or booby trap. Although IEDs are as old as explosives, it is only in the 21st century that they have become a significant — perhaps the most significant — characteristic of warfare, as warfare itself has changed to become overwhelmingly asymmetric and low intensity.

Cake tins and Coke cans

Early medieval Chinese gunpowder weapons included forms of IED, with bamboo tubes stuffed with gunpowder and shrapnel. The value of IEDs as a response to both armor and infantry was quickly appreciated by the First World War soldiers who improvised anti-tank and personnel mines by using grenades and even cake tins stuffed with explosives (see page 175). During the Vietnam War, one of the US military's first experiences with insurgency warfare, the Viet Cong noticed that US soldiers tended to kick empty soda cans they found along the road, and took to hiding IEDs inside them. IEDs have also been used by terrorists dating back to the Irish Republican Army (IRA) and beyond. In 1996, for instance, Eric Rudolph set off a homemade pipe bomb at the Atlanta Olympics, killing one person and injuring 100 others.

But IEDs have had by far their greatest impact in the post-9/11 conflicts in Iraq and Afghanistan. In Afghanistan in 2011, for instance, over 50 percent of NATO casualties were caused by IEDs, and IEDs accounted for one in three Afghans killed that year, whereas from January to November 2012, according to

the NATO-led International Security Assistance Force (ISAF) in Afghanistan, IEDs caused more than 70 percent of civilian casualties. In Iraq, according to the Iraq Body Count website, 41,636 civilians were killed by explosives between March 20th, 2003, and March 14th, 2013. In the two conflicts combined, IEDs have killed more than 3,100 US troops and wounded 33,000 others. IEDs are also increasingly common outside these two war zones: in the 12 months from September 2012, there were more than 15,000 IED explosions outside Afghanistan, according to the Joint Improvised Explosive Device Defeat Organization (JIEDDO). "[IEDs] have caused us a lot of pain," recognizes US Army Lt. Gen. John Johnson, who leads JIEDDO. "It costs us a lot of effort, and a lot of treasure, to counteract the effects of those weapons systems, [and] protect our forces."

Anatomy of an IED

IEDs come in many shapes and sizes , but most have the following components in common. A power supply, such as a battery, supplies

power to a trigger or switch of some sort, which sets off a detonator or fuse. This in turn sets off the main charge, which may be packed in and surrounded by euphemistically termed "enhancements" such as glass, nails, or metal fragments. The whole bomb is packed in a container, which will also fragment on detonation. The main charge may be military explosives, such as C4, homemade explosives such as ANFO (a mixture of ammonium nitrate, which acts as the oxidizer, and fuel oil, which is the fuel source), or repurposed ordnance such as an old landmine, unexploded artillery shell, hand grenade, and so on. "It is difficult to fight these devices," says Franco Fiore, a counter-IED (C-IED) specialist at the NATO Consultation, Command and Control Agency. "Detonation may be triggered by command, a time switch, or a booby trap. They may be buried underground, or camouflaged to merge with the surroundings." A common technique is to use a mobile phone as the switch to set off roadside bombs; the trigger man observes traffic from a concealed location, and when he spots a target he dials a number to set off the IED. A lower-tech alternative is simply a wire leading from the fuse to a battery, with the IED set off by touching two wires together.

However, it is a mistake to think that IEDs are simply primitive devices thrown together by uncoordinated amateurs. These devices can be sophisticated in construction, and the multilayer network behind them involves technicians, trainers, supply chains, and financiers. The trigger man is often at the bottom of the "food chain" — a simple farmer or herdsman paid a handful of dollars to dig a hole and watch for targets.

Countering IEDs

The prominence of IEDs as the primary weapon used against NATO forces has prompted a massive C-IED effort, developing techniques and technologies from jammers and scanners to sniffer dogs and extensive counterintelligence programs. JIEDDO, for instance, has spent nearly $25 billion on equipment to protect troops, train them, and target bomb-making networks since 2006. One of the most visible C-IED responses has been the use of increasing numbers of Mine Resistant Ambush Protected (MRAP) vehicles, armored trucks with V-shaped bottoms to divert blast waves. Most ISAF vehicles in Afghanistan are now fitted with jamming devices. According to Franco Fiore, "The jammer deafens the IED receiver by

"Homemade explosives now account for almost all of the improvised explosive devices in Iraq. They are easy to make, simple to use, and the costs are minimal."

GENERAL HADI SALMAN, HEAD OF MILITARY ENGINEERING AT THE IRAQI MINISTRY OF DEFENSE, 2013

A bomb-sniffing dog named Krash searches for IEDs in a suspicious rock pile on the roadside; Afghanistan, 2009.

shouting louder than the transmitter or talking over it." Other devices include NIRF (neutralizing improvised explosive devices with radio frequency), which emits a high-frequency radio pulse to deactivate IED electronics over a short range; microwave-pulsing devices that "fry" IED electronics remotely; and LIBS (laser-induced breakdown spectroscopy), where lasers are used to detect explosives within a 100-foot (30 m) radius. Despite all this technology, sniffer dogs remain the most effective way of detecting IEDs.

A lot of work is now being done to prevent IED attacks from happening in the first place, by targeting the networks behind them. According to Colonel Santiago San Antonio Demetrio, director of the C-IED Center of Excellence, "Training in combating IEDs is principally focused on the ability to counter the networks before they put the devices in place." To this end, the US has been quietly amassing a huge library of IED remains and components, at the FBI Lab's Terrorist Explosive Device Analytical Center (TEDAC). A warehouse on the outskirts of Washington, D.C. archives the remnants of 100,000 explosive devices gathered over the last 10 years, with about 800 new ones arriving every month from Afghanistan and 20 other countries. TEDAC looks for fingerprints, common components and techniques, and other traces of individual bomb-makers, and is said to have identified more than 1,000 of them.

NATO Secretary General Anders Fogh Rasmussen announced at a press conference in 2012, "In Afghanistan, we have learned how important it is to protect our forces against roadside bombs. So a number of Allies will jointly acquire remote-controlled robots which can clear such bombs — protecting our forces and civilians alike." This will entail a considerable long-term investment, considered of vital importance.

IMPROVISED EXPLOSIVE DEVICE (IED)

49

Inventor(s):

British Royal Navy

UNMANNED AERIAL VEHICLE (UAV) DRONES

Social ■

Political ■

Tactical ■

Technical ■

Type:

Unmanned aerial vehicles (UAVs)

21st century

"Drone" is a generic name for a pilotless vehicle; drones can include boats and land vehicles, but by far the most common type is the unmanned aerial vehicle (UAV — although the Pentagon, the main developer and buyer of drones, prefers the term "unmanned aerial system," UAS). Drones are not robots, although they are commonly described as such — robots are autonomous and responsive, whereas all drones are currently remotely controlled or programmed. The dividing lines between them, however, are blurring (see page 214).

Tesla's telautomatons

Drones may seem like the stuff of science fiction but they have been transforming the nature of warfare for over a decade. The best-known UAV, the Predator, was named by Smithsonian's *Air & Space* magazine as one of the top 10 aircraft that changed the world. The Pentagon currently has nearly 11,000 aerial drones, and more than one in three military aircraft is now a drone (albeit the majority of these are small Raven drones, each of which weighs just 4.2 pounds/1.9 kg). This represents a colossal increase over a very short time: in 2005 only 5 percent of US military aircraft were drones; drones almost certainly now outnumber manned aircraft in the American military. Investment in drones is set to increase still further: the Pentagon plans to spend almost $24 billion on unmanned air, ground, and maritime systems up to the end of 2018.

Drones have a surprisingly long history. Although it was not appreciated or understood at the time, one of the first public demonstrations of radio, by Nikola Tesla at the Electrical Exposition in Madison Square Gardens in 1898, featured what were possibly

A US soldier launches a Raven in Iraq in 2006; the most popular military UAV in the world, the Raven is used for reconnaissance and surveillance.

the first radio-controlled vehicles, and thus the first drones: boats that Tesla called "telautomatons." These ran off wirelessly transmitted power and had sophisticated control systems of lights and motors enabling them to perform complex operations, but only in response to correctly coded broadcasts on multiple frequencies.

During the First World War British inventor Harry Grindell Matthews successfully marketed to the Royal Navy a remote-controlled boat technology based on selenium, a metal that generates electricity when illuminated. He used selenium in a relatively simple remote-control technology, creating a boat called *Dawn* that could be remotely controlled by a beam of light carrying what Grindell Matthews described as "pulsations of sufficiently rapid frequency to be invisible to the eye." Equipped with a "selenium pilot," this small boat could be steered and operated with the beam of a searchlight, and he eventually got it to work at ranges of up to 3,000 yards (2.7 km) in "diffused daylight" and 5 miles (8 km) at night. Although the British military bought the technology, it was never developed further.

Queen Bees and Hellcats

The Second World War era saw both sides developing radio-controlled aircraft, such as the German Argus As 292, the British Queen Bee, and American TDR drones, which carried 1.1-ton (1 tonne) bombs to drop on enemy shipping. The US Air Force fitted remote controls to F6F Hellcat planes packed with 2,000-pound (907 kg) bombs to create kamikaze drones that were used to take out targets during the Korean War. In the 1960s and 1970s the US military used the AQM-34 Ryan Firebee drone for reconnaissance, but the primary antecedents of high-profile modern drones such as the Predator were the light Scout and Pioneer glider-style drones developed by the Israelis in the 1970s and 1980s.

Drone technology development may have had unintentional consequences, as in the case of the SPRITE: in the 1970s Westland helicopters designed for the military a stealth unmanned mini-copter, the Surveillance Patrol Reconnaissance Intelligence Target Designation Electronic Warfare, or SPRITE, which could carry thermal imaging cameras, lasers, and

Ryan Firebee drones mounted on the wing of a Hercules; the Firebee was one of the first widely used UAVs, developed as a target drone for gunnery practice.

> "I have a brother who's an Army Special Forces. And honestly I wouldn't want him stepping out the door without this thing [a Reaper drone] over the top of him."

LIEUTENANT COLONEL CHRIS GOUGH, REAPER PILOT, 2009

other hi-tech payload. SPRITE was deemed responsible for many UFO sightings in Wiltshire, England, in the early 1980s when it was being tested on top-secret night flights.

A huge capability

The logic of UAVs has come to seem inescapable to the military, especially the US military. Compared to conventional aircraft, UAVs are much cheaper, more expendable, easier to transport and deploy, and use less fuel. Crucially, they also keep operating personnel out of harm's way. Many American Predator and Reaper (a larger armed drone) missions, for instance, are controlled from a facility at Creech Air Force Base near Las Vegas. The drone's "pilots," controlling the craft via satellite link-ups, can fly combat missions, blow up suspected terrorists and insurgents, and then drive home to the suburbs for dinner with the family. This surreal set-up is reportedly resulting in high levels of operator stress, but it is also changing the nature of 21st-century warfare in ways that are far more stressful to America's enemies. In a 2009 interview with CBS News, Colonel Chris Chambliss, commanding the drone unit at Creech, pointed out the benefits:

When we can take 34 airplanes, and we can have them airborne all the time, and they can look at whatever we need them to look at, that's a huge capability and so because of that, the enemy has to do things differently now. They have to hide more. They don't know when we're looking at 'em. They don't know where we are.

Future directions for UAVs include longer flying and more capable versions of existing technology; increasingly small, cheap, and disposable micro-UAVs to equip individual foot soldiers with personal reconnaissance tech; and an increasing drive to weaponize drones. A recent Pentagon report, *Unmanned Systems Integrated Roadmap: FY2013–2038*, states: "Adapting proven weapons technology with new concepts to take advantage of unmanned systems persistence and emerging net-centric capability, manned and unmanned teaming will be critical to improving the sensor-to-shooter equation and further decreasing in the kill chain timeline." In other words, the military will increasingly kill by remote control.

UNMANNED AERIAL VEHICLE (UAV) DRONES

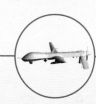

UAV Drones

[A] Communications antenna
[B] Synthetic aperture radar unit
[C] Camera sensory array
[D] Wings (48.5 feet/14.8 m across)
[E] Push propellor
[F] Hellfire missiles

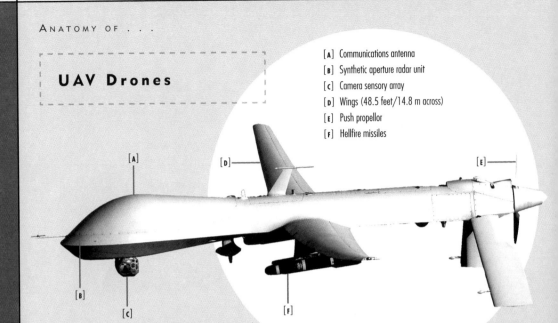

The best-known UAV drone is the Predator, with a 48.7-foot (14.8 m) wingspan, a push-propeller medium-altitude, long-range aircraft. Its makers, General Atomics Aeronautical, describe it as "the most combat-proven Unmanned Aircraft System in the world." The Predator can fly at up to 25,000 feet (7,600 m) and stay aloft for 40 hours (24 hours fully loaded). It is used both in reconnaissance mode, and, when armed with munitions such as Hellfire missiles, as a combat strike aircraft (designated the MQ-1). The Predator has become increasingly important to the US military. First flown in 1994, it took until 2007 for the Predator fleet to accumulate 250,000 flight hours, but just another 20 months to rack up 500,000 hours.

The combat MQ-1 Predator has been controversially used in a program of stealthy aerial assassination, such as the November 3rd, 2002 CIA attack in the Yemen in which a Hellfire missile launched from a Predator took out Qaed Senyan al-Harthi, the al-Qaeda leader thought to be responsible for the bombing of the USS *Cole*. "The Predator has become central to the way we operate," General Norton Schwartz, the Chief of Staff of the Air Force, told CBS's *60 Minutes*, "[it] is probably at the head of the line [in terms of] damage to al-Qaeda."

KEY FEATURE:

WHAT'S IN A NAME?

The manufacturers of the Predator are concerned that the common term "drone" is pejorative, with overtones of mindlessness that do not sit well with lethal strike capabilities, and even that "unmanned aerial vehicle/system" fails to reflect properly the key element of the Predator system — the operators. For this reason the term "remotely piloted vehicle" is now officially preferred.

In Iraq, for instance, Predator operator teams typically consisted of a pilot and a sensor operator working at the air base from which the UAV launched and touched down, who would work to ensure that take-off and landing went smoothly. Once airborne, control of the Predator was passed on to operator teams working very remotely — from air bases in the United States, controlling the drone by satellite.

50

Inventor(s):

Boston Dynamics

ROBOTS

Type:

Autonomous machine system

Social ■
Political ┄
Tactical ■
Technical ■

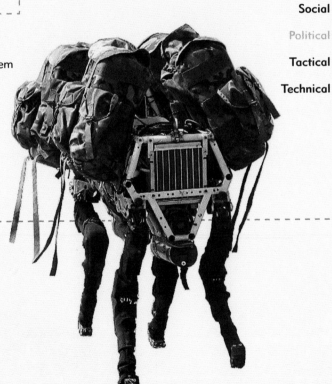

The Future

Imagine a war where the only combatants are machines. Fast, agile androids with articulated, tentaclelike appendages sprint between cover, coordinating their advance through constant short-range communication and "swarm" algorithms that build overarching patterns of behavior from individual unit feeds. Much larger, tracked armored machines loaded with heavy artillery rumble up behind them. Overhead, swarms of small autonomous fliers feed surveillance data to the ground units, simultaneously acquiring their own targets. The firing starts and destruction rains down; at no point has a human been involved.

The robot myth

This is the scenario imagined since science-fiction writers first seized upon the concept of robots almost a century ago, and which has now become common cultural currency through films such as *The Terminator* and *The Matrix*.

If the public perception of current military technology, fed by lazy journalistic clichés, were accurate, such a scenario would be just around the corner, for it is widely accepted that robots have already transformed warfare and are soon to take over altogether. In fact, the truth is very different: although robots may, in the near to medium future, have profound logistical and moral impact on the conduct of warfare, they are very far from doing so now.

The most persistent myth about military robots is that robots are already in service; this arises from a simple misunderstanding of the meaning of the term "robot." Although drones such as the Predator and other UAVs are typically termed robots, this is inaccurate. A robot is an autonomous machine: one that can perform a task, however simple, without human control or guidance. The most common type of robot in the world is the automobile assembly line robot: an articulated arm that can follow a precise program of motions and actions on its own. A drone, on the other hand, is not autonomous; it is piloted by remote control. Some drones, such as NASA's Mars Rover *Curiosity*, are capable of limited autonomy — given a series of way points, it can work out how to get from one to the other and deal with the intervening terrain. But few military drones approach even this level of autonomy.

The devices most commonly described as military robots are unmanned ground vehicles (UGVs) typically used for anti-explosives work, such as inspecting for or defusing IEDs. UGVs in use by NATO and allies include TALON, PackBot, MATILDA, and ACER. These are all tracked vehicles, with broad, low profiles, although ACER is larger than the others and is essentially an unmanned bulldozer. Such UGVs can act as platforms for other technology, such as robotic arms, cameras and other sensors, and firefighting equipment. TALON units armed with different types of weapon including machine guns and grenade launchers, known as

SWORDS (special weapons observation reconnaissance detection system), were first trialed in the early 2000s and a small number were sent to Iraq in 2007, but they were never used in the field. Like UAVs, however, UGVs are not robots — they are remote-controlled drones, operated by soldiers within fairly short range.

The trouble with robots

So why are the military not equipped with robots, decades after science-fiction writers and futurists assured us they would be commonplace? The fault lies not with the military, but with a fundamental failure in the science of robotics. Simply put, robots have proved to be too hard to make.

Mechanical automatons featured in myths and legends as far back as Homer's *Odyssey*. Real versions have been devised as entertainments and curiosities since ancient times, but the word "robot" itself has a much more recent origin, having been coined in 1921 by Czech playwright and futurist Karel Čapek. Čapek adapted the Czech word *robota*, meaning "serf" or "laborer," for his play *Rossum's Universal Robots*, about a factory owner who builds himself an automated workforce. True robots did not arrive until 1956, when engineer Joseph Engelberger and inventor George Devol

A Talon "robot" (in reality a remote-controlled ground vehicle) is readied for deployment by a bomb-disposal engineer during a "Best Sapper" competition in 2010.

"It is very hard to develop a robot to do special operations, but we have already replaced sentries on the DMZ [Korean Demilitarized Zone] with semi-autonomous systems."

ARIZONA STATE UNIVERSITY ENGINEERING PROFESSOR BRADEN ALLENBY, 2014 formed Unimation, the world's first robotics company. Together, they developed the world's first industrial robot, the Unimate, a cranelike device with a grasping "hand" on the end. In 1962 the Unimate went to work on a General Motors production line in Trenton, New Jersey, lifting and stacking hot metal plates. Commercially available robots have not advanced that far beyond the Unimate, because the challenges that face truly autonomous robots have proved daunting.

Humans and other animals take for granted the ability to sense and negotiate complex dynamic environments, interact robustly with them, and power and maintain themselves efficiently. Getting machines to do any of these things has so far proved almost impossible. One of the major problems has been the difficulty of developing artificial intelligence (AI) that can approach even rudimentary animal sentience. Lightweight but long-lasting power packs have also been problematic, as has robust design and engineering that can survive outside the laboratory environment. Difficulties in overcoming these challenges has led to the commonplace joke that "robots are 20 years away, and always will be."

AlphaDog

There is at least one true robot, however, that is very close to entering military service. Boston Dynamics (BD) is a robotics company that draws inspiration from animal biomechanics to design walking robots that have become well known through internet exposure. The best-known of these is the quadrupedal Big Dog,

partly funded by the military research agency DARPA, which in turn has given rise to the AlphaDog, or the L3 Legged Squad Support System, a robotic "pack mule" that can carry up to 400 pounds (181 kg) for up to 20 miles (32 km) over 24 hours, negotiating tough terrain and righting itself if it falls. A related prototype from BD is the WildCat, a fast-moving quadrupedal robot that can run at speeds of up to 15.5 mph (25 kph).

These are true robots, in that they are autonomous and require no control by human operators (although they do take instruction, following simple commands such as "stay" and "follow," and are able to shadow a human "master" at a constant distance). AlphaDog has been in development since 2005, and has yet to undergo full field trials. The challenge to making it field-ready is indicated by comments made by BD co-founder Marc Raiberto in November 2013: "When the project started a few years ago, the 'mean time to failure' [for AlphaDog] was just 0.5 hour. Now they've improved that to 3.4 hours."

Although it could be a few years until AlphaDog or other truly autonomous robots are ready to enter service, when they do there is the obvious potential that, like the TALON SWORDS, they could be fitted with armaments. Allowing autonomous machines to make decisions about firing and killing would open up a new and troubling world of ethical dilemmas.

FURTHER READING

Arthur, Max (2005) *Last Post: The Final Word from our First World War Soldiers*, London: Weidenfeld & Nicolson

Bidwell, Shelford and Dominick Graham (2004) *Fire Power: The British Army Weapons and Theories of War 1904–1945*, Barnsley: Leo Cooper Ltd

Bodley Scott, Richard, Nik Gaukroger and Charles Masefield (2010) *Field of Glory Renaissance: The Age of Pike and Shot*, Oxford: Osprey

Brodie, Bernard (1959) *Strategy in the Missile Age*, Princeton: Princeton University Press

Brodie, Bernard and Fawn M. Brodie (1973) *From Crossbow to H-Bomb: The Evolution of the Weapons and Tactics of Warfare*, Bloomington, IN: Indiana University Press

Campbell, Christy (2012) *Target London: Under Attack from the V-weapons during WWII*, London: Little, Brown

Chambers, John Whiteclay II, ed. (1999) *The Oxford Companion to American Military History*, Oxford: Oxford University Press

Chun, Clayton K.S. (2006) *Thunder Over the Horizon: From V-2 Rockets to Ballistic Missiles*, Westport, CT: Praeger Publishers

Cooper, Jonathan (2008) *Scottish Renaissance Army 1513–1550*, Oxford: Osprey

Cowley, Robert and Geoffrey Parker, eds. (1996) *The Osprey Companion to Military History*, Oxford: Osprey

Croll, Mike (1998) *The History of Landmines*, Barnsley: Pen & Sword Books Ltd

Dear, I.C.B. and Peter Kemp, eds. (2005) *Oxford Companion to Ships and the Sea*, Oxford: Oxford University Press

Dear, I.C.B. and M.R.D. Foot, eds. (2005) *The Oxford Companion to World War II*, Oxford: Oxford University Press

Delbrück, Hans (1990) *The Dawn of Modern Warfare (History of the Art of War, Volume IV)*, trans. by W. J. Renfroe, Lincoln, NE: University of Nebraska Press

Forczyk, Robert A. (2007) *Panther Vs T-34: Ukraine 1943*, Oxford: Osprey

Gillespie, Paul G. (2006) *Weapons of Choice: The Development of Precision Guided Munitions*, Tuscaloosa, AL: University of Alabama Press

Hardy, Robert (1976) *Longbow: A Social and Military History*, Cambridge: Stephens

Holmes, Richard, ed. (2001) *The Oxford Companion to Military History*, Oxford: Oxford University Press

Keegan, John (2004) *The Face of Battle: A Study of Agincourt, Waterloo and the Somme*, London: Pimlico

Keegan, John and Richard Holmes (1985) *Soldiers: A History of Men in Battle*, London: Hamish Hamilton

Levy, Joel (2012) *History's Worst Battles: And the People Who Fought Them*, London: New Burlington

Liddell Hart, B. H. (1959) *The Tanks: The History of the Royal Tank Regiment and its Predecessors*, London: Cassell

Liddell Hart, B. H. (1973) *The Other Side of the Hill: The Classic Account of Germany's Generals, Their Rise and Fall, with Their Own Account of Military Events, 1939-1945*, London: Cassell

Loades, Mike (2010) *Swords and Swordsmen*, Barnsley: Pen & Sword Military

MacGregor, Neil (2012) *A History of the World in 100 Objects*, London: Penguin

Macksey, Kenneth (1976) *Tank Warfare: A History of Tanks in Battle*, St. Albans: Panther

Manucy, Albert C. (2011) *Artillery Through the Ages: A Short Illustrated History of Cannon*, Leonaur

McNab, Chris (2011) *A History of the World in 100 Weapons*, Oxford: Osprey

McNab, Chris (2011) *The Uzi Submachine Gun*, Oxford: Osprey

Moynihan, Michael, ed. (1973) *People at War 1914–1918*, Newton Abbot: David and Charles

Nicholson, Helen J. (1997) *The Chronicle of the Third Crusade: A Translation of the Itinerarium Peregrinorum et Gesta Regis Ricardi (Crusade Texts in Translation)* Aldershot, England: Ashgate

Popenker, Maxim and Anthony G. Williams (2011) *Sub-machine Gun: The Development of Sub-machine Guns and Their Ammunition from World War 1 to the Present Day*, Ramsbury: Crowood Press

Rhodes, Richard (1988) *The Making of the Atomic Bomb*, London: Penguin

Rottman, Gordon L. (2011) *The AK-47: Kalashnikov-series Assault Rifles*, Oxford: Osprey

Simpson, John (2009) *Strange Places, Questionable People*, London: Pan Macmillan

Singer, P. W. (2011) *Wired for War: The Robotics Revolution and Conflict in the 21st Century*, London: Penguin

Stanford, Dennis J. and Bruce A. Bradle (2013) *Across Atlantic Ice: The Origin of America's Clovis Culture*, Berkeley, CA: University of California Press

Tonsetic, Robert L. (2010) *Days of Valor: An Inside Account of the Bloodiest Six Months of the Vietnam War*, Havertown, PA: Casemate

Tucker, Spencer C., ed. (2009) *A Global Chronology of Conflict: From the Ancient World to the Modern Middle East*, Santa Barbara, CA: ABC-CLIO

Turnbull, Stephen (2002) *World War I Trench Warfare (1): 1914–16*, Oxford: Osprey

Vale, Malcolm (1981) *War and Chivalry: Warfare and Aristocratic Culture in England, France and Burgundy at the End of the Middle Ages*, London: Duckworth

White, Lynn (1962) *Medieval Technology and Social Change*, Oxford: Clarendon Press

Wills, Chuck (2006) *An Illustrated History of Weaponry: From Flint Axes to Automatic Weapons*, London: Carlton

USEFUL WEBSITES

Ancient Chinese Military Technology: *http://depts.washington.edu/chinaciv/miltech/miltech.htm*

Army Technology: *www.army-technology.com*

The Association for Renaissance Martial Arts: *http://thearma.org*

British Battles: *http://britishbattles.com*

Browning (gunsmiths): *www.browning.com*

Chuck Hawks Naval, Aviation and Military History: *www.chuckhawks.com/index3.naval_military_history.htm*

De Re Militari, The Society for Medieval Military History: *http://deremilitari.org*

Defense Tech: *http://defensetech.org*

Encyclopaedia Romana: *http://penelope.uchicago.edu/~grout/encyclopaedia_romana/index.html*

Engineering the Medieval Achievement: *http://web.mit.edu/21h.416/www/index.html*

Evolution of Modern Humans: *http://anthro.palomar.edu/homo2/default.htm*

Eyewitness to History: *http://eyewitnesstohistory.com*

The Garand Collectors Association: *http://thegca.org*

Historic Arms Resource Centre: *http://rifleman.org.uk*

Illustrated History of the Roman Empire: *http://roman-empire.net*

International Campaign to Ban Landmines: *http://icbl.org*

Internet History Sourcebook Project, Fordham University: *www.fordham.edu/Halsall/index.asp*

The Lee Enfield Rifle Association: *www.leeenfieldrifleassociation.org.uk*

Military History magazine: *www.historynet.com/magazines/military_history*

myArmoury: A Resource for Historic Arms and Armour Collectors: *www.myarmoury.com*

The Napoleon Series: *http://napoleon-series.org*

North Atlantic Treaty Organization (NATO): *www.nato.int*

Naval History and Heritage Command: *www.history.navy.mil*

Prehistoric Archery and Atlatl Society: *www.thepaas.org*

The Roman Military Research Society: *http://romanarmy.net*

Spartacus Educational: *www.spartacus.schoolnet.co.uk/index.html*

The Great War – WWI Battlefields and History: *www.greatwar.co.uk*

World Guns: *http://world.guns.ru*

Xenophon Group: *http://xenophongroup.com*

IMAGE CREDITS

8 © BabelStone | Creative Commons

9 top © Mercy from Wikimedia Commons | Creative Commons

9 bottom © Didier Descouens | Creative Commons

10 © Michel wal | Creative Commons

12 © jason cox | Shutterstock.com

14 © Daderot | Creative Commons

15 © Eric Gaba | Creative Commons

16, 19 © Creative Commons

20 © Daderot | Creative Commons

24 © INTERFOTO | Alamy

25 © Dbachmann | Creative Commons

27 © Getty Images

31 © Luis García | Creative Commons

32 © Mary Evans Picture Library

35 © Library of Congress | public domain

36 © duncan1890 | iStockphoto

39 © Library of Congress | public domain

41 © INTERFOTO | Alamy

43 © Ivy Close Images | Alamy

44 © oksana2010 | Shutterstock.com

55 © INTERFOTO | Alamy

61 © Mary Evans Picture Library | THE TANN COLLECTION

64 Library of Congress | public domain

66 © Getty Images

68 © UIG via Getty Images

69 © UIG via Getty Images

70 © HiSunnySky | Shutterstock.com

72 © Lee Sie | Creative Commons

77 © Time & Life Pictures | Getty Images

78 © Getty Images

82 © Kallista Images | Getty Images

84 CDC/James Hicks | public domain

86 © Dan Kosmayer | Shutterstock.com

94 © Hein Nouwens | Shutterstock.com

101 © Illustrated London News Ltd | Mary Evans

108 © Getty Images

110 © Morphart Creation | Shutterstock.com

111 Library of Congress | Public Domain

112 © Aleks49 | Shutterstock.com

115 © Illustrated London News Ltd | Mary Evans

119 © Erwin Franzen | Creative Commons

120, 123 © Stocktrek Images, Inc. | Alamy

123 bottom © Topory | Creative Commons

124 © Jean-Louis Dubois | Creative Commons

126 © Minnesota Historical Society | Creative Commons

127 Library of Congress| public domain

129 © Otis Historical Archives National Museum of Health & Medicine | Creative Commons

132, 137 © AlfvanBeem | Creative Commons

138 © David Orcea | Shutterstock.com

139 © Jamie C | Creative Commons

141 © Getty Images

142 © Rama | Creative Commons

145 © Alf van Beem | Creative Commons

146 © TRINACRIA PHOTO | Shutterstock.com

150 © Andrei Rybachuk | Shutterstock.com

152 © UIG via Getty Images

156 © Bundesarchiv, Bild 146-1973-029A-24A | Lysiak | Creative Commons

158 © SSPL via Getty Images

166 © mashurov | Shutterstock.com

169 top © zimand | Shutterstock.com

170 © zimand | Shutterstock.com

174 © Wiskerke | Alamy

178 © Stephen Saks | Getty Images

184 © zimand | Shutterstock.com

188 © Imperial War Museums (FIR 9263)

200 © Gamma-Rapho via Getty Images

203 © US Navy | Creative Commons

204 © Smitt | iStockphoto

214 © AlamyCelebrity | Alamy

INDEX